NATIONAL AUDUBON SOCIETY®

FIRST FIELD GUIDE

INSECTS

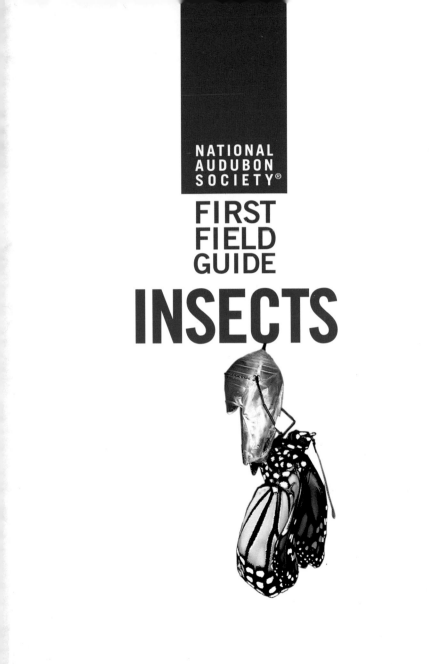

NATIONAL AUDUBON SOCIETY®

FIRST FIELD GUIDE

INSECTS

Written by

Christina Wilsdon

Scholastic Inc.

New York Toronto London Auckland Sydney
Mexico City New Delhi Hong Kong

595.7

The National Audubon Society, established in 1905, has 550,000 members and more than 500 chapters nationwide. Its mission is to conserve and restore natural ecosystems, focusing on birds and other wildlife, and these guides are part of that mission. Celebrating the beauty and wonders of nature, Audubon looks toward its second century of educating people of all ages.

For information about Audubon membership, contact:

National Audubon Society

700 Broadway

New York, NY 10003-9562

800-274-4201

http://www.audubon.org/

LIBRARY OF CONGRESS CATALOGING-IN-PUBLICATION DATA
Wilsdon, Christina.
  National Audubon Society first field guide to insects/Christina Wilsdon.
    p. cm.
  Includes index.
  Summary: A visual guide to the natural science of insects, which includes information on the ten most common orders, pollination, and life cycles; also works as a field guide.
ISBN 0-590-05483-X ISBN 0-590-05447-3
1. Insects—juvenile literature. 2. Insects—North America—Juvenile literature.
[1. Insects.] I. National Audubon Society.
II. Title.
QL467.2.W57 1997
595.7—dc21 97-17990 CIP AC

ISBN 0-590-05447-3 (HC)
ISBN 0-590-05483-X (PB)

10 9 8 7 6 5 4 3 2 1   0/0   01   02

Printed in Hong Kong
First printing, April 1998

National Audubon Society® is a registered trademark of National Audubon Society, Inc., all rights reserved.
Front cover photograph: Praying Mantis *(Mantis religiosa)* by Michael Lustbader/Photo Researchers, Inc.

Contents

The world of insects
About this book   6
What is a naturalist?   8
A world full of insects   10
How old are insects?   12
What is an arthropod?   14
Insect or...spider?   16
Name that insect   18

How to look at insects
Telling insects apart   20
Telling more insects apart   22
Meet the beetles   24
Flies   26
True bugs   28
Bees, wasps, and ants   30
Social insects   32
Crickets and grasshoppers   34
Dragonflies and damselflies   36
Butterflies and moths   38
Growth and metamorphosis   40
Mantids, roaches, earwigs, and mayflies   42
Spiders   44
Endangered insects   46

Field guide
Using the field guide   48
Field guide   50

Reference
How to use the reference section   150
Glossary   150
Resources   152
Index   154
Credits   158

About this book

Orange Sulphur

Whether you are looking at insects in your own backyard, taking a vacation by a lake, or hiking through an alpine meadow, this book will help you see insects the way a naturalist does. The book is divided into four parts:

Part 1: The world of insects tells you how naturalists learn about insects, where insects live, how long they have existed, what other creatures are like them, how insects and spiders differ, and how insects are named.

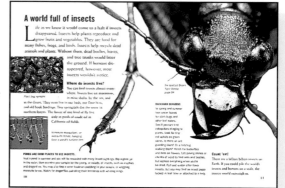

A world full of insects

Life as we know it would come to a halt if insects disappeared. Insects help plants reproduce and grow fruits and vegetables. They are food for many fishes, frogs, and birds. Insects recycle dead animals and plants. Without them, dead bodies, leaves, and tree trunks would litter the ground. If humans disappeared, however, most insects wouldn't notice.

Where do insects live?
You can find insects almost everywhere. Insects live on mountains, in snow shafts by the sea, and in the desert. They even live in our beds, our floor hairs, and old book bindings. They spring-tails live the snow in northern forests. The larvae of one kind of fly live only in pools of crude oil in California oil fields.

Fast-bug vignette

[illustrations of aquatic insects] mosquito, or mosquito larva, hanging from a pond's surface film

PONDS ARE GOOD PLACES TO SEE INSECTS.
You'd pond in summer and and will be rewarded with many insect sightings. Dip a glass jar in the water, then examine your sample for the young, or nymphs, of insects, such as mayflies and dragonflies. You may also find a water boatman paddling in your sample, or wriggling mosquito larvae. Watch for dragonflies patrolling their territories with whirring wings.

Six-spotted Tiger Beetle page 54

BACKYARD DENIZENS
In spring and summer, leaves unfurl from plants for plant bugs and other leaf-eaters. See if you can find caterpillars clinging to plants. Look for tiny red aphids on green stems. Is there an ant guarding them? Or a ladybug stalking them? Watch for butterflies and bees on flowers. Lift paving stones or chunks of wood to find ants and beetles, but explore everything where you've looked. Each and water after have insects, but you may find an insect pupa tucked in leaf litter or attached to a twig.

Count 'em!
There are a billion billion insects on Earth. If you could pile the world's insects and humans on a scale, the insects would outweigh us.

Part 2: How to look at insects gives you the information you need to begin identifying insects in the field; provides fascinating facts about the twelve groups of insects you are most likely to see; explains their life cycles; and describes the plights of several rare and endangered species.

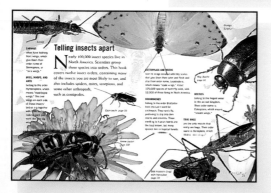

Telling insects apart

Nearly 100,000 insect species live in North America. Scientists group these species into orders. This book covers twelve insect orders, containing many of the insects you are most likely to see, and also includes spiders, mites, scorpions, and some other arthropods, such as centipedes.

BEES, WASPS, AND ANTS
belong to the order Hymenoptera, which means "membrane wings." This two-wings-on-each-side of these insects' bodies zip together with tiny hooks. Scientists make work-like the tiny wings...

Earwig

EARWIGS
often have feathery front wings, which give them their order name of Dermaptera, or "skin wings."

Cockroach page 56

CATERPILLARS AND MOTHS
soar on wings covered with tiny scales that give them their color and flash and also have order name, Lepidoptera, which means "scale wings." About 175,000 species of butterfly exist, with 12,000 of these living in North America.

Orange Sulphur

COCKROACHES
belong to the order Blattodea from the Latin word for cockroach. They rarely fly, preferring to slip into their cracks and crevices. These cockroach is human haunts are the food lobster, but many species live in tropical forests.

BEETLES
belong to the largest order in the animal kingdom. Their order name is Coleoptera, which means "sheath wings."

May Beetle page 52

TRUE BUGS
are the only insects that really are bugs. Their order name is Hemiptera, which means "one-wings."

Bonne Jacket page 100

Bow Boston Snap with Herculae page 36

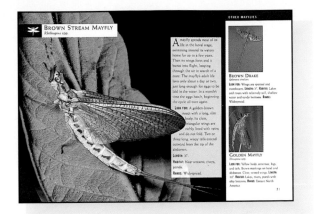

Part 3: The field guide includes detailed descriptions, range maps, and dramatic photographs of 50 common North American insects, spiders, and other arthropods. This section also provides shorter descriptions and photographs of 125 other important species.

Part 4: The reference section at the back of the book includes a helpful glossary of technical terms used by entomologists and naturalists; lists of useful books, organizations, videotapes, software, and Web sites; and an index of species covered in the field guide.

What is a naturalist?

Jean-Henri Fabre,
French entomologist

When you see an insect on a leaf, do you look at it closely? Do you wonder what it is? A naturalist studies nature to understand how it works. You don't need to be a scientist to study nature, and you don't have to travel to a far-off rain forest—a world of wonders waits in your own backyard. All you need is curiosity and the ability to spot clues and ask questions.

What is an entomologist?

An entomologist is a scientist who studies insects. Like naturalists, entomologists watch, listen, and record what they see. Jean-Henri Fabre was a French entomologist who lived from 1823 to 1915. He didn't kill and mount insects in order to study them, as many other scientists did. Instead he observed how insects behaved in the places where they lived.

A naturalist's tools

Here are helpful tools for
studying insects: a magnifying
glass; a plastic "bug box"; tweezers
to pick up insects gently; field guides, like this
one, to help you identify insects; a journal, pens,
and pencils to record your observations in words
and drawings; and a camera to take pictures.

Rules for a naturalist

- Always explore with a buddy, and make sure an adult
  knows where you're going and what you're doing.
- Some insects sting. Never touch or pick up an insect
  unless you know what it is.
- Pick up insects gently. You can get an insect to crawl onto a leaf or twig
  without touching it. Always put insects back where you found them.
- If you turn over a rock, put it back where you found it.
- If you put an insect in a container, make sure there are air holes in it.
- Stay off private property unless you have permission to be there.
- Don't litter! Leave nature the way you found it.

A world full of insects

Life as we know it would come to a halt if insects disappeared. Insects help plants reproduce and grow fruits and vegetables. They are food for many fishes, frogs, and birds. Insects help recycle dead animals and plants. Without them, dead bodies, leaves, and tree trunks would litter the ground. If humans disappeared, however, most insects wouldn't notice.

Plant bug nymphs

Where do insects live?

You can find insects almost everywhere. Insects live on mountains, in mine shafts, by the sea, and in the desert. They even live in our beds, our flour bins, and old book bindings. Tiny springtails dot the snow in northern forests. The larvae of one kind of fly live only in pools of crude oil in California oil fields.

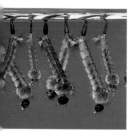

Immature mosquitoes, or mosquito larvae, hanging from a pond's surface film

PONDS ARE GOOD PLACES TO SEE INSECTS.

Visit a pond in summer and you will be rewarded with many insect sightings. Dip a glass jar in the water; then examine your sample for the young, or naiads, of insects, such as mayflies and dragonflies. You may also find a water boatman paddling in your sample, or wriggling mosquito larvae. Watch for dragonflies patrolling their territories with whirring wings.

*Six-spotted Green
Tiger Beetle
page 84*

BACKYARD DENIZENS

In spring and summer
look under leaves
for stink bugs and
other leaf eaters.
See if you can find
caterpillars clinging to
plants. Look for tiny
red aphids on green
stems. Is there an ant
guarding them? Or a ladybug
stalking them? Watch for butterflies
and bees on flowers. Lift paving stones or
chunks of wood to find ants and beetles,
but replace everything when you're
finished. Fall and winter offer fewer
insects, but you may find an insect pupa
tucked in leaf litter or attached to a twig.

Count 'em!

There are a billion billion insects on
Earth. If you could pile the world's
insects and humans on a scale, the
insects would outweigh us.

11

How old are insects?

Insects have existed for at least 350 million years—about 120 million years before dinosaurs appeared. The first insects were probably wingless and much like today's silverfish. Over time, insects developed wings—long before other creatures took to the air.

American Cockroach page 56

Silverfish

Ancient insects

Fossils of insects are rare. The soft body of an insect normally rots too quickly to form a fossil. But there are cases in which prehistoric insects were buried in mud that later turned to rock. Prints of the insects' bodies and wings were left in the rock. Scientists have found fossils of 300-million-year-old dragonflies with 30-inch wingspans—the largest insects that have yet been found.

A modern dragonfly resting on a giant fossil dragonfly

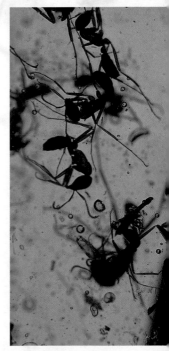

Tree traps

If you check the sticky liquid oozing from a pine tree, you might see small insects trapped in it. Insects that lived 100 million years ago also got caught in this liquid, called resin. Over time, the resin hardened into transparent lumps of amber, preserving the insects inside.

This 40-million-year-old grasshopper caught in amber closely resembles its modern cousins.

Ants in amber

13

What is an arthropod?

Touch your ribs. What you're feeling is your skeleton—the bones that keep your body from collapsing. Arthropods, including such animals as insects, centipedes, and arachnids (spiders, scorpions, mites, and ticks), wear their skeletons outside. This outer skeleton, or exoskeleton, covering the arthropod's soft insides is made of a tough material called chitin.

Arthropods' bodies are divided into sections. In fact, *arthropod* means "joint legs."

Insects Most known arthropods are insects. They have six legs, three main body parts, one or two pairs of wings, and two antennae. About a million insects have been identified. Some scientists think there may be ten million or more species yet to be discovered.

Red Milkweed Beetle page 95

Goldenrod Spider
page 139

Arachnids

Spiders, scorpions, ticks,
and mites are all arachnids.
They have eight legs and
only one or two main
body sections. They don't
have antennae.
Arachnids form the
second-largest class
of arthropods.

Scorpion page 144

Wood Tick
page 146

Centipedes

Centipedes are hunters that feed on worms,
snails, and insects. The biggest centipedes,
which may be as long as 13 inches, go after
lizards and even mice. Centipedes, with one
pair of legs on each body segment, are often
confused with millipedes, another class of
arthropods with two pairs of legs on each body
segment. Centipedes kill their prey with a pair
of claws that release a paralyzing venom.

Hermit Crab

Centipede
page 148

Crustaceans

This class includes lobsters, shrimps, and
crabs. Most crustaceans live in water.
They have two pairs of antennae
on their heads.

Beautiful Tiger Beetle page 85

Insect or...

I f an arthropod has
three main body sections, six
legs, and two antennae, it is an insect.
An insect's three body sections are the head,
the thorax, and the abdomen, and each of
these is divided into smaller segments.

● Mandibles

THE MANDIBLES
are a pair of jaws
that open and
close from side
to side. Used for
cutting, chewing,
grasping, and
crushing, they lie
on each side of
an insect's mouth.

THE ANTENNAE
are for touching,
tasting, and
smelling.

● Antennae

● Head

THE HEAD
contains the insect's
brain. Also on its
head are a pair of
antennae, one to
three simple eyes,
each with a single
light-sensitive unit,
and two compound
eyes, each with many
light-sensitive units.

THE THORAX
is divided into
three segments,
with a pair of
jointed legs
attached to
each one.

● Thorax

*Cow Killer Wasp
(female)*

● Abdomen

THE ABDOMEN
contains most of the
heart and digestive
system. It also holds
the reproductive
organs. If the insect
stings, this is where
the poison glands
are found.

16

...spider?

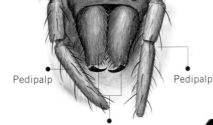

Pedipalp   Pedipalp

Chelicerae

I f the arthropod you are looking at has two main body sections, eight legs, and no antennae or wings, it is an arachnid—most likely a spider.

THE PEDIPALPS help the spider catch, hold, and crush its prey.

THE CHELICERAE are a spider's jaws. They are equipped with fangs that inject venom.

THE CEPHALOTHORAX is made up of both the head and thorax combined. (These two parts are separate in an insect.) A spider's eight legs are attached to the cephalothorax.

Silver Argiope

• Cephalothorax

• Abdomen

THE ABDOMEN contains the spider's heart, some of its digestive system, and its reproductive organs.

Black-and-yellow Garden Spider, page 138

SILK WEBS, LININGS, AND PURSES

Beneath a spider's abdomen and near its tip are spinnerets. These little stubs are used to spin silk made inside the spider's abdomen. Some spiders spin webs with the silk. Others use silk to line burrows. Many make silk bags for their eggs.

17

Name that insect

Harlequin Cabbage Bug
Scientific Name:
Murgantia histrionica
page 71

Gulf Fritillary

If a friend says, "There's a bug on your shirt," do you picture a few different kinds of insects? Scientists avoid such confusion by using two-part scientific names for insects. If your pal had said, "There's a *Murgantia histrionica* on your sleeve," an insect scientist would know that your visitor was a Harlequin Cabbage Bug—a black-and-orange stink bug that sucks the juices of cabbage, broccoli, and other crops.

BACK BASICS

One way to classify animals is by whether or not they have backbones. People, snakes, frogs, and canaries do and are called vertebrates. Animals without backbones are called invertebrates. This group includes insects, jellyfish, worms, snails, and many others.

18

Names and more names

Animals are classified, or divided, by scientists into groups, and each one has a name. The largest group is called a kingdom. The animal kingdom includes all animals—you, your dog, insects. Kingdoms are separated into phyla. Each phylum is broken down into classes. Each class is arranged in orders, which are sorted into families. A family is divided into genera (plural of *genus*), which are again divided into species.

WHERE DO SCIENTIFIC NAMES COME FROM?

An insect's scientific name is usually in Latin. The first word tells you what genus of insects it belongs to; the second name identifies what species it belongs to. A species is made up of animals that mate and produce fertile young. A scientist who discovers a new species gets to name it. The species name may reveal where the animal lives or what it looks like. It may even be a person's name—maybe that of a scientist's best friend!

Ebony Jewelwing page 54

FIVE CREATURES CLASSIFIED

	HUMAN	GORILLA	DOG	HONEYBEE	AMERICAN LOBSTER
KINGDOM	Animal	Animal	Animal	Animal	Animal
PHYLUM	Chordata	Chordata	Chordata	Arthropoda	Arthropoda
CLASS	Mammalia	Mammalia	Mammalia	Insecta	Crustacea
ORDER	Primate	Primate	Carnivora	Hymenoptera	Decapoda
FAMILY	Hominidae	Pongidae	Canidae	Apidae	Homaridae
GENUS	*Homo*	*Gorilla*	*Canis*	*Apis*	*Homarus*
SPECIES	*sapiens*	*gorilla*	*familiaris*	*mellifera*	*americanus*
	(Humans are the only species in the genus *Homo*.)				

Riparian Earwig

EARWIGS
often have leathery front wings, which give them their order name of Dermaptera, or "skin wings."

BEES, WASPS, AND ANTS
belong to the order Hymenoptera, which means "membrane wings." The two wings on each side of these insects' bodies zip together with little hooks, making each pair work like one big wing.

Telling insects apart

Nearly 100,000 insect species live in North America. Scientists group these species into orders. This book covers twelve insect orders, containing many of the insects you are most likely to see, and also includes spiders, mites, scorpions, and some other arthropods, such as centipedes.

American Cockroach page 56

Yellow Jacket page 132

Orange
Sulphur

BUTTERFLIES AND MOTHS

soar on wings covered with tiny scales
that give them their color and flash and
also their order name, Lepidoptera, which
means "scale wings." About 125,000
species of butterflies and moths exist;
12,000 live in North America.

May Beetle
page 91

COCKROACHES

belong to the order Blattodea
from the Latin word for
cockroach. They rarely fly,
preferring to slip into thin
cracks and crevices. Those
dwelling in human homes are
the best known, but many
species live in tropical forests.

BEETLES

belong to the largest order
in the animal kingdom.
Their order name is
Coleoptera, which means
"sheath wings."

TRUE BUGS

are the only insects that
really are bugs. Their order
name is Hemiptera, which
means "half wings."

Bee Assassin (bug)
with Honeybee
page 73

21

Mayfly page 50

MAYFLIES

belong to the order Ephemeroptera, which means "short-lived wings," referring to the brief life of the adult mayfly. Some mayflies live for a few days, while others live for just a few hours.

MANTIDS

can not be confused with any other insects! These long, lean, bug-eyed hunters use their front legs to snatch other insects. They belong to the order Mantodea.

Praying Mantis page 58

Telling more

DRAGONFLIES AND DAMSELFLIES

skim across waterways looking for other insects to eat. These hunters belong to the order Odonata, which means "tooth jawed."

Green Darner page 52

CRICKETS AND GRASSHOPPERS have strong hind legs for jumping. They belong to the order Orthoptera, which means "straight wings." Over 23,000 species hop worldwide; North America has about 1,000 species.

Southeastern Lubber Grasshopper

insects apart

CICADAS, leafhoppers, and aphids all dine on plants. These insects are part of the order Homoptera, which means "similar wings."

SPIDERS are not insects, but with 3,000 species of them living in North America, you will likely see them as you look for insects. They belong to the order Araneae.

Goldenrod Spider page 139

FLIES, MOSQUITOES, GNATS, AND MIDGES belong to the order Diptera, which means "two wings." Unlike most other insects, which have four wings, they have only two. The other set is reduced to a pair of little knobs.

Mosquito page 104

Periodical Cicada page 76

23

Meet the beetles

There are more kinds of beetles than any other kind of animal in the world. You'll find beetles almost anywhere—in forests and deserts, on beaches and mountains, in the air and in water, even in hot springs.

Convergent Ladybug Beetle page 94

Always hungry

A single ladybug may gobble up to 5,000 aphids during its life. Their ravenous appetites for pests make ladybugs favorites with gardeners.

Tortoise Beetle

THE ELYTRA are a beetle's two hard front wings. Tucked beneath them are two soft hind wings. (Only one of the elytra is visible from this angle.)

Eastern Hercules Beetle

CLEARLY A BEETLE
The top wings,or elytra, of the leaf-eating Tortoise Beetle are clear, allowing its brown-and-yellow body to show through. The name Tortoise comes from its habit of yanking its antennae under its "shell" when frightened.

Ladybug taking off with elytra extended

Getting a lift

When a beetle flies, it lifts its elytra, holds them away from its body, and flaps its uncovered flying wings. The elytra don't flap, but they do provide extra lift.

THE PRONOTUM is the shield-like top of the first section of the thorax. It covers the first pair of a beetle's six legs.

Clean-up crews

Small dead creatures are feasts for Tomentose Burying Beetles. Using their antennae, these orange-and-black insects can find a mouse within an hour of its death, from as far away as two miles. Working in pairs, they

Tomentose Burying Beetle

bury the corpse, mate, and lay eggs in the grave. The carcass provides nourishment for hatching larvae.

A MASSIVE HORN sticks out from the male Eastern Hercules Beetle's pronotum. The Hercules Beetle looks fierce, but it eats mainly leaves. It uses its horn for fighting with other males over females.

Flies

Soldier Fly

Flies are insects people love to hate, and the order Diptera, meaning "two wings," includes some of the most annoying and dangerous insects, such as House Flies and disease-carrying mosquitoes. However, flies are important to the environment. They are major sources of food for birds, bats, and fish. Next to bees and wasps, they are the main pollinators of flowers.

AERIAL ACROBATS

If the insect you're looking at has only two wings, it is probably a fly. Most insects have four wings; flies have only two. Flies can hover in one spot like a hummingbird. Some can even fly backward.

A fly's foot magnified 125 times

FLY EYES

Each of a fly's two compound eyes consists of as many as 4,000 tiny units called ommatidia. Each unit works like a miniature eye, seeing just a bit of the total picture. A fly's compound eyes don't produce a sharp image, but they sense motion well.

A fly's head magnified 24 times

FORMIDABLE FEET

A fly can walk vertically or even upside down on any surface. Each foot

A fly's foot magnified 56 times

has a pair of sharp claws that hook into pits and bumps on the surface (invisible to us but visible to a fly). Each foot also has a sticky, hairy pad that gives a fly a no-slip grip.

BLOODTHIRSTY MOMS

Over 90,000 fly species flit around the world, including mosquitoes, crane flies, gnats, and midges. When a mosquito or black fly bites you, it pierces your skin and then sucks your blood. The biter is always a female; she needs blood to provide protein for her eggs.

Female mosquito page 104

Giant Water Bug (page 69) attacking a frog

True bugs

Green Stink Bug page 70

This Green Stink Bug has glands on its underside from which it can squirt a smelly liquid if disturbed.

Many people use the word "bug" to mean just about any insect. But scientists reserve the term "true bug" for insects with front wings that are thick and tough at the base, yet delicate and see-through toward the tips. Such wings give true bugs the name of their order— Hemiptera, which means "half wings."

The Giant Water Bug (above) is among our largest insects; some grow over two inches long.

Dogday Harvestfly (a cicada) molting page 77

Slurp!

Between meals, a true bug keeps its beak under its head, pointing backward. When the bug eats, it pulls the beak forward. Inside are four mouthparts. The sharp outer two stab plants or animal skin. The inside pair fit together to form two tubes. Digestive juices flow through one tube, and the bug sucks up food through the other.

Bug-like—but not really bugs

Cicadas, treehoppers, and aphids belong to an insect order called Homoptera, which means "similar wings." The homopterans are like true bugs in some ways. They have stabbing, sucking mouthparts, but these are located farther back on the head and point downward. Also, the wings of a homopteran are filmy and light—without any tough, leathery parts. Homopterans feed on plants, not animals. One homopteran, the treehopper, has a pointy thorax that looks like a thorn on a branch.

Treehopper page 79

GROWING UNDERGROUND

The molted skins of cicadas can often be seen stuck to tree trunks. Cicadas hatch in trees and drop to the ground as nymphs. They burrow into the soil and feed on juices in roots, growing and molting for a year or more. One species takes 17 years to mature!

29

Bees, wasps, and ants

Mud-dauber Wasp

The ants at your picnic, the wasp in your backyard, and the bee buzzing on a wildflower are members of the order Hymenoptera, meaning "membrane wings." The buzz is made by four tiny wings flapping furiously. But you won't hear worker ants, of course. They don't have wings.

Bumblebee
page 137

WASP WAISTS
Bees, wasps, and ants can wiggle their hind ends freely, thanks to their narrow waists, called pedicels. In some wasps and ants, the pedicel is very long and thin.

Yellow Jacket
page 132

Wasps

Adult Yellow Jacket wasps drink sweet liquids, such as nectar, but they feed chewed up insects to larvae. Some wasps paralyze insects with their stingers, stuff them into the ground, then lay eggs on the bodies. The larvae that hatch will eat the disabled insects.

OUCH!

Many wasps, bees, and ants can sting. Millions of years ago, their stingers were egg-laying tubes. Over time, the tubes evolved into sharp lances with poison sacs.

Paper Wasps feeding larvae
page 133

Bees

Bees are the most important pollinators. As they buzz among flowers, they carry pollen from one plant to another. Bees visit flowers to gather pollen or nectar, the sweet liquid made by plants. With long mouthparts, they reach into pockets of nectar tucked within a flower's petals.

Ants

Fire Ant page 135

The worker ant scurrying across your floor isn't a lone explorer. She reports back to hundreds or thousands of sisters after she finishes searching for food. Many ants gather tidbits—dead insects, seeds, and cookie crumbs, for example. Others hunt insects, collect seeds, or even snip leaves and use them for growing a crop of fungi to eat.

31

Social insects

Social insects live together, with each individual working to help the whole group survive. Workers have strong bonds with each other and toil for a common ruler, the queen.

Wasp ways

Most wasps live on their own, but some live in groups. A Yellow Jacket queen starts a colony by laying eggs that hatch into workers. The Yellow Jacket visiting your picnic is a female worker, looking for food to bring back to larvae. Workers also make the nest bigger by chewing wood into a mushy paste and using it to build more egg chambers.

Cross section of a Paper Wasp nest

Ants smelling each other by touching antennae

Lots of ants, few uncles

An ant colony consists of hundreds or thousands of female workers and one queen. Males die after mating. Workers care for the queen, tend her eggs, feed larvae, collect food, dig tunnels, and defend the nest. At times the workers feed a few ant larvae extra food; these become new queens that leave the nest to mate and form new colonies.

Carpenter Ant worker page 135

There's no place like comb.

Honeybees live in colonies made up of a queen, some males, and many female workers. A colony may contain 80,000 workers, who raise the young, build combs out of beeswax to hold the larvae and honey, gather nectar and pollen, make the honey, and guard the nest. Worker bees live about six weeks, while a queen may last five years. Workers that hatch in the fall, however, survive the winter. They huddle inside the nest for warmth, dining on stored honey.

Honeybees on a comb

33

Crickets and grasshoppers

Field Cricket page 66

I n many parts of North America, the sounds of summer include the chirping of crickets and grasshoppers. These insects have long, strong hind legs made for jumping and jaws designed for chewing on plants. Most also have a pair of thin, strong front wings, with a second pair folded up like fans beneath. But some members of the order Orthoptera don't have any wings at all.

Southeastern Lubber Grasshopper chewing on a flower petal

MAKING MUSIC

Crickets are the songbirds of the insect world, but usually only males chirp and trill to attract females and to warn other males away. Crickets or long-horned grasshoppers make music by scraping a sharp part of one wing against a file-like part on its other wing. Short-horned grass-hoppers often buzz by rubbing their hind legs or wings against their front wings. Because crickets have shorter wings than grasshoppers, their songs have a higher pitch and sound nicer to human ears.

Leaping short-horned grasshopper

Take a leap

The femur, or top part of a cricket's or grasshopper's leg, bulges with muscles and provides the power for its mighty leaps. The tibia, or lower part, is thin and straight. The insect folds up its long hind legs and presses the spiny spurs of its feet against the surface it's standing on before leaping.

Femur   Tibia

THE LONG AND SHORT OF IT
The antennae of a short-horned grasshopper are rarely half the length of the insect's body. A long-horned grasshopper has antennae as long or longer than its body. The two grasshoppers also have hearing organs in different places. A short-horned grasshopper's hearing organs are on the sides of its abdomen. A long-horned grasshopper has flat, round ears near the "knee" of each of its front legs.

35

Dragonflies and damselflies

Watch by a pond in summer, and you are bound to see dragonflies and damselflies zip by. These agile, flying hunters snatch mosquitoes and other insects out of the air by scooping them up with their long, bristly legs. Then they clutch their prey tightly while slicing them into bits with their jaws. With their bright, flashing colors, many dragonflies and damselflies look like flying jewels.

NIMBLE FLIERS

Dragonflies and damselflies flap their front pair of wings separately from their hind pair. They can change direction in a flash, hover, and fly backward. Some dragonflies zip along at 35 miles per hour while catching other flying insects.

Damselfly

Dragonfly

Which is which?

It's easy to tell a dragonfly from a damselfly. At rest, all dragonflies hold their wings straight out to their sides. Resting damselflies hold their wings above their backs, pointing to the rear or at an angle. Damselflies are thin and delicate-looking. Dragonflies tend to be bigger and bulkier. They are also stronger, faster fliers.

*Twelve-spot
Skimmer
(a dragonfly)*

Mating dance

Dragonflies and damselflies mate while flying. Then the females lay their eggs in water or on plants. While a female is laying her eggs, the male may clutch her behind her head with claspers at the tip of his abdomen. The two often fly through the air attached in this way.

*Male damselfly clasping
female laying eggs*

Dragonfly naiad

WATER BABIES

A dragonfly or a damselfly starts life as a water creature called a naiad. A naiad carries its mask-like lower lip folded up under its head most of the time—until it spots a small fish, an insect, or a tadpole. Then it thrusts its lip forward quickly, snares the prey with sharp hooks, and drags the meal to its mouth.

Butterflies and moths

Monarch page 118

Spangled, striped, and spotted, butterflies dazzle our eyes as they flit through the air. Most of their duller kin, the moths, fly by night and hide during the day. But

Io Moth

some moths possess brilliant wings. The Luna Moth, for example (see next page), flaps in the night on ghostly aqua-green wings four inches wide.

Butterfly or moth?

How do you tell a butterfly from a moth? Most butterflies hold their wings together over the back when resting. A moth generally holds its wings spread out over its body or curled up tightly around it. A butterfly's antennae are generally long, with knobs at the end. A moth's antennae lack knobs, are usually shorter, and may be fuzzy.

Zebra butterfly's coiled proboscis

Tongue twirled

Most butterflies and moths have a coiled-tube mouthpart called a proboscis. It works like a straw, sucking up nectar, tree sap, and fruit juice. Some moths drink tears that bathe animals' eyes.

LONG-DISTANCE CHAMPION

Like many birds, the butterfly known as the Monarch migrates south for the winter. Eastern and midwestern Monarchs fly all the way to Mexico. Western Monarchs fly to forests along California's coast. In spring, the Monarchs head north to lay eggs. The adults die, but their young finish the journey north.

Butterfly garden

You can attract butterflies to your yard by planting the flowers they dine on. Daisies, lilacs, snapdragons, cosmos, and yarrow are common garden plants that lure butterflies. Butterflies will also flock to "butterfly bushes," which are called Buddleia and grow orange, white, blue, pink, or purple flowers. Find a sunny spot, then plant what will grow well in your area.

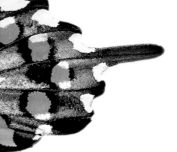

Pipevine Swallowtail

EATING MACHINES

Moths and butterflies undergo complete metamorphoses (see pages 40–41). Eggs are laid on plants that the larvae (caterpillars) eat. Some caterpillars have big spots that look like eyes and help startle predators. Others have sharp spines to protect themselves.

Cecropia Moth caterpillar

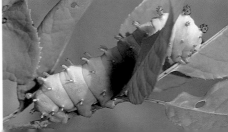

Growth and metamorphosis

Silverfish

An insect generally goes through a process called metamorphosis as it grows from hatchling to adult. Because its skin, or exoskeleton, can't change size, an insect molts, or sheds its skin. When an insect's new skin is fully developed, the old one splits, and the insect crawls out.

Simple growth

A few insects, such as the silverfish, hardly change from one molt to the next. The young insect, or nymph, looks like a tiny adult and just keeps molting until it is fully grown.

Incomplete metamorphosis

Nymphs of some insects, such as bugs, look like small adults without wings. After each molt, the nymphs resemble their parents more. But they don't get full sets of wings or sex organs until a final molt.

A STINK BUG MOLTING

The three pictures at the right show a molting Green Stink Bug. In the near picture, the bug begins to split out of its immature, darkly striped skin. In the middle picture, the bug has nearly shed the old skin. In the far picture, the bug walks away from its old skin.

Soldier Fly

Complete metamorphosis

Wasps, bees, beetles, moths, flies, and butterflies go through changes called complete metamorphosis. The larva (young insect) looks very different from the adult. After molting a few times, the larva transforms into a pupa. During this stage the exoskeleton acts as a protective case. Inside, the larva's body breaks down and reassembles itself. Eventually an adult struggles out.

40

A Monarch caterpillar about to change into a pupa, or chrysalis

A Monarch beginning to break out of its chrysalis

Metamorphosis of a Monarch

After molting several times, a Monarch caterpillar suspends itself from a milkweed leaf

A Monarch caterpillar eats milkweed leaves.

on a silken cord, sheds its skin, and changes into a pupa, or chrysalis. Ten days later the green chrysalis becomes clear, and you can see the adult butterfly inside.

Its wings are crumpled and soft when it breaks out. Once they expand and harden, the butterfly flies away.

An adult Monarch, newly emerged from its chrysalis.

41

Mantids, roaches, earwigs, and mayflies

Common Earwig

People admire mantids because they eat pests, but many dislike earwigs because they eat flowers. Cockroaches are unpopular, too, because they invade our homes. Mayflies live so short a time, most people don't even know they exist.

*Mayfly
page 50*

Eerie insects?

It was once believed that earwigs crawled into people's ears to lay their eggs. That's how this insect got its name. The story isn't true, but it is a fact that earwigs' smooth, flat bodies are perfectly made for slipping into narrow spaces.

A very short life

An adult mayfly doesn't need to eat—it will live only a few hours or days. The male mates, then dies. The female lives only long enough to lay her eggs. The order name, Ephemeroptera, means "short-lived wings." On the other hand, the mayfly larva enjoys a long life. It may live for one to four years underwater, eating algae and tiny particles of food.

42

American Cockroach
page 56

Praying Mantis
page 58

Uninvited guests

Many kinds of cockroaches live in buildings. Their flat bodies, with which they hid from predators 350 million years ago, now help them hide from people. The insects find their way in the dark with their long antennae, which also detect air currents. Tropical roaches eat decaying plants and animals. House roaches make do with crumbs.

Fierce feeder

A Praying Mantis is almost always a *preying* mantis—on the alert for insects passing by. The mantid watches with huge eyes mounted on a head that twists and turns freely. Four long hind legs grip leaves and twigs. Its long, folded front legs, armed with spikes, are like coiled springs waiting to snap shut on hapless prey.

Spiders

Spiders aren't insects; they're members of an arthropod group called arachnids. A spider injects venom with its fangs, then releases saliva, turning a victim's insides into a liquid, which it drinks.

Arrow-shaped Microthena

A TARANTULA UP CLOSE

Like other spiders, a tarantula has two body sections, eight legs, and a head located on its front body part. It uses its two fangs to puncture and hold prey while its leg-like pedipalps squeeze out body juices. A tarantula's bite can be painful, but it isn't any more dangerous than a bee sting.

CLOSE, BUT NO SPIDER

A Daddy-long-legs isn't a spider, though it looks a lot like one. It doesn't have a waist between its front body part and its abdomen. Its legs are longer and thinner than a spider's, and it carries its body hung low. Daddy-long-legs eat insects and worms, and some kinds also eat fungi and rotting fruit.

Daddy-long-legs page 141

Silken strands

Golden-silk Spider

Under a spider's abdomen, near the rear, are tiny stubs called spinnerets. The spider uses its legs to pull liquid silk made in its abdomen from the spinnerets. The silk hardens as it stretches. Since silk is made out of protein, a spider eats the used silk of an old web before spinning a new one.

Wolf Spider carrying an egg sac

Versatile silk

Not all spiders spin webs, but many use silk in other ways. Some protect their eggs in silken egg sacs. The Wolf Spider carries her egg sac attached to her spinnerets. Many tarantulas line their burrows with silk. Some trap-door spiders make silken lids for their burrows.

Desert Tarantula page 143

FANGS

PEDIPALPS

45

Endangered insects

Endangered Tiger Beetle

The most serious threats to insects, such as this endangered tiger beetle, are the destruction of their habitats, the use of pesticides, and pollution. Many people, however, are working hard to stop practices that harm insects. They urge farmers to use pesticides that kill only certain insect pests. People are also working to pass laws that will protect habitats. Such laws help not only insects, but also other animals and plants.

Mitchell's Satyr

GOING WITH THE TERRITORY

The Mitchell's Satyr lives in fens, or wetlands. Over time, fens have been drained to make way for farms and houses. As fens have become more scarce, so has the Mitchell's Satyr. Unfortunately, the butterfly's rareness has not stopped collectors from catching it. Now the species lives only in North Carolina and a few areas near the Great Lakes.

Oregon Silverspot

HAUNTED NO MORE

The Ringed Bog Haunter is a rare dragonfly that lives in boggy parts of New England. Long ago, swamps filled with white cedar trees were very common in New England. But people drained the swamps so they could cut down the trees. As a result of the destruction of its habitat, the Ringed Bog Haunter all but disappeared. Today, white cedar swamps are protected places.

Ringed Bog Haunter

VANISHING WITH SEASIDE MEADOWS

The Oregon Silverspot butterfly lives only in meadows near the coast—places that are popular with people, too. Many such meadows have been "developed"—cleared and replaced with houses and businesses. Stopping the paving and plowing of coastal grasslands will save the habitat of this beautiful butterfly.

Using the field guide

This section features 50 common North American insects, spiders, and other arthropods plus 125 more, with photographs and descriptions of each. Generally, species on facing pages are similar in

Red Milkweed Beetle page 95

some way; sometimes they belong to the same family. The letters *spp.* following a name means that the species is one of several similar species in the same genus.

Eastern Hercules Beetle

ICONS

These icons identify a creature's general shape and category.

Mayflies, Dragonflies, & Damselflies	**Grasshoppers & Crickets**	**Butterflies & Moths**
Cockroaches & True Bugs	**Fleas, Springtails, & Lice**	**Social insects**
Mantids & Walkingsticks	**Beetles**	**Arachnids**
Cicadas, Dobsonflies, & Kin	**Flies**	 **Centipedes, Millipedes, & Sowbugs**

SHAPE ICON

This icon identifies the featured insect's general shape and category.

NAME

The common and scientific names appear here.

BOX HEADING

The heading alerts you to the other insects or arthropods covered in the box, which are similar in some way to the main one on the page. These box headings include: Other Mayflies, Other Dragonflies, Other Damselflies, Look-alikes, Similar Species, In the Same Family, Other Arachnids, Other Scorpions, and more.

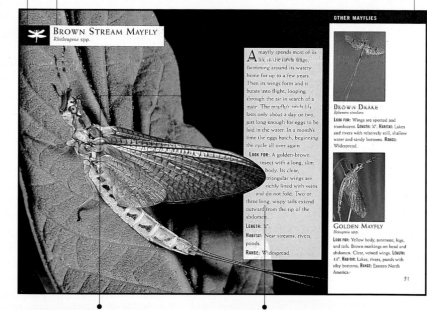

OTHER MAYFLIES

BROWN STREAM MAYFLY
Rhithrogena spp.

A mayfly spends most of its life in the larval stage, swimming around its watery home for up to a few years. Then its wings form and it bursts into flight, looping through the air in search of a mate. The mayfly's adult life lasts only about a day or two, just long enough for eggs to be laid in the water. In a month's time the eggs hatch, beginning the cycle all over again.

LOOK FOR: A golden-brown insect with a long, slim body. Its clear, triangular wings are richly lined with veins and do not fold. Two or three long, wispy tails extend outward from the tip of the abdomen.
LENGTH: ½".
HABITAT: Near streams, rivers, ponds.
RANGE: Widespread.

BROWN DRAKE
Ephemera simulans
LOOK FOR: Wings are spotted and translucent. **LENGTH:** ¾". **HABITAT:** Lakes and rivers with relatively still, shallow water and sandy bottoms. **RANGE:** Widespread.

GOLDEN MAYFLY
Hexagenia spp.
LOOK FOR: Yellow body, antennae, legs, and tails. Brown markings on head and abdomen. Clear, veined wings. **LENGTH:** 1⅛". **HABITAT:** Lakes, rivers, ponds with silty bottoms. **RANGE:** Eastern North America.

51

IDENTIFICATION CAPSULE

The identification capsule covers the details you need to identify an insect or other arthropod: color, size, parts of the body, and other field marks described in Part 2 of this book.

HABITAT AND RANGE

The habitat and range listings tell you whether or not an insect, spider, or other arthropod is likely to be in your area.

BROWN STREAM MAYFLY

Rhithrogena spp.

A mayfly spends most of its life in the larval stage, swimming around its watery home for up to a few years. Then its wings form and it bursts into flight, looping through the air in search of a mate. The mayfly's adult life lasts only about a day or two, just long enough for eggs to be laid in the water. In a month's time the eggs hatch, beginning the cycle all over again.

LOOK FOR: A golden-brown insect with a long, slim body. Its clear, triangular wings are richly lined with veins and do not fold. Two or three long, wispy tails extend outward from the tip of the abdomen.

LENGTH: ⅝".

HABITAT: Near streams, rivers, ponds.

RANGE: Widespread.

BROWN DRAKE
Ephemera simulans

LOOK FOR: Wings are spotted and translucent. **LENGTH:** ⅞". **HABITAT:** Lakes and rivers with relatively still, shallow water and sandy bottoms. **RANGE:** Widespread.

GOLDEN MAYFLY
Hexagenia spp.

LOOK FOR: Yellow body, antennae, legs, and tails. Brown markings on head and abdomen. Clear, veined wings. **LENGTH:** 1⅛". **HABITAT:** Lakes, rivers, ponds with silty bottoms. **RANGE:** Eastern North America.

51

GREEN DARNER
Anax junius

Nicknamed "Darning Needle," the Green Darner's needle-thin body seems dwarfed by its magnificent wings. The breadth of its wingspan helps to explain why this insect is one of the fastest-flying dragonflies.

LOOK FOR: A large dragonfly with a green thorax, violet-blue abdomen, and clear wings.

LENGTH: 2¾–3⅛".

HABITAT: Ponds, streams, fields.

RANGE: Widespread; more common in the East.

COMMON WHITETAIL
Libellula lydia

LOOK FOR: Gray-brown thorax with white or yellow spots; dark band near wing tip. Male: white abdomen. Female: brown with yellow spots. **LENGTH:** 1⅞". **HABITAT:** Near ponds, streams. **RANGE:** Widespread.

HALLOWEEN PENNANT
Celithemis eponina

LOOK FOR: Amber head and body; yellow wings with brown bands and spots. **LENGTH:** 1⅝". **HABITAT:** Borders of weedy ponds. **RANGE:** East of the Rockies.

RED SKIMMER
Libellula saturata

LOOK FOR: A red dragonfly with brown on head and brownish-red thorax. Yellowish wings with red veins. **LENGTH:** 2⅜". **HABITAT:** Ponds, marshes. **RANGE:** Mostly the South; also found north to Montana.

53

EBONY JEWELWING
Calopteryx maculata

Even more needle-like than the Green Darner, this damselfly is named for its black wings. But what is truly spectacular about this insect is its gleaming, metallic-green body. When not in flight, the Ebony Jewelwing holds its wings together vertically above its body, not spread out as dragonflies do.

LOOK FOR: The male's body is metallic green with black wings; the female's body is dark brown with smoky white-tipped wings.

LENGTH: 1¾".

HABITAT: Slow-moving rivers and streams.

RANGE: Widespread.

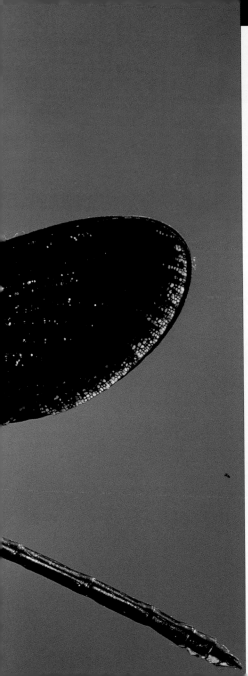

DOUBLEDAY'S BLUET
Enallagma doubledayii

LOOK FOR: A bright blue damselfly with black bands on thorax and abdomen. Clear wings. **LENGTH:** 1¼". **HABITAT:** Ponds, bogs, swamps. **RANGE:** East Coast.

EASTERN FORKTAIL
Ischnura verticalis

LOOK FOR: Male: black thorax with two lime-green stripes; black abdomen with blue tip. Female: blue-gray or orange; clear wings. This is New England's most common damselfly. **LENGTH:** 1". **HABITAT:** Ponds, streams, rivers. **RANGE:** East.

55

AMERICAN COCKROACH
Periplaneta americana

Also called a "Waterbug," the American Cockroach can fly, as well as escape on foot into cracks in our homes. It stays hidden by day, but at night goes out in search of food (which includes just about everything).

LOOK FOR: A flattened, reddish-brown body with a pale yellow head shield; very long antennae.

LENGTH: 1½–2".

HABITAT: Moist, dark crevices in vegetation and buildings.

RANGE: Florida to Mexico; Antarctica to Greenland.

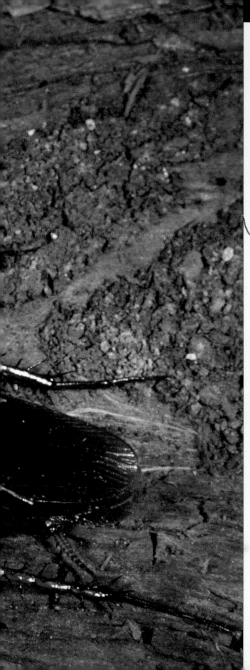

GERMAN COCKROACH
Blatella germanica

LOOK FOR: A light to dark brown body with two brown lines along upper part of thorax. Sticky pads on feet enable this insect to walk up slick surfaces without falling. **LENGTH:** ⅝". **HABITAT:** Homes, restaurants, factories where food is processed. **RANGE:** Widespread.

ORIENTAL COCKROACH
Blatta orientalis

LOOK FOR: A dark reddish-brown and black cockroach. Slightly larger than the German Cockroach. **LENGTH:** 1". **HABITAT:** Buildings, especially those in which food is stored. **RANGE:** Throughout North America.

57

PRAYING MANTIS
Mantis religiosa

NORTHERN WALKINGSTICK
Diapheromera femorata

LOOK FOR: A very slow moving, long, thin insect that looks like a twig. It is wingless, and its color may change from brown to green or green to brown. The walkingstick can grow new legs to replace lost ones. **LENGTH:** 3¾". **HABITAT:** Leafy forests. **RANGE:** East of the Rockies.

CAROLINA MANTID
Stagmomantis carolina

LOOK FOR: Light green and pale grayish-brown, this mantid blends in with woody stems and other vegetation. **LENGTH:** 2⅜". **HABITAT:** Shrubs, gardens. **RANGE:** Southern half of United States.

This skilled hunter waits with its front legs folded, as if praying for an insect to stray within its deadly grasp. The mantid's flexible neck allows it to swivel its head as it looks for prey.

LOOK FOR: A long, narrow, green or tan body with a triangle-shaped head. The two front legs are larger than the others; underneath each is a black-edged white spot.

LENGTH: 2–2½".

HABITAT: Brushy fields, gardens.

RANGE: Eastern United States and southeastern Canada.

59

COMMON STONEFLY
Family *Perlidae*

Common Stoneflies spend most of their adult lives near water, resting under bridges or sitting on stones. At dusk in the summer, they can be seen swarming about in a mating "dance."

LOOK FOR: A narrow insect with two antennae and two stiff hairs resembling antennae at the rear. The hind wings fold flat under the fore wings, covering almost the whole abdomen.

LENGTH: ⅜–1⅝".

HABITAT: Cold streams and lakes.

RANGE: Widespread.

GIANT STONEFLY
Family *Pteronarcidae*

LOOK FOR: A large stonefly with gray wings. Can be seen at night clustering around outdoor lamps. **LENGTH:** 2½". **HABITAT:** Near freshwater lakes, ponds, rivers. **RANGE:** Widespread.

GREEN-WINGED STONEFLY
Family *Perlodidae*

LOOK FOR: A greenish-yellow insect with green-tinged wings. The upper third of the thorax, known as the pronotum, is somewhat rectangular. **LENGTH:** ⅝". **HABITAT:** Near streams, lakes, ponds. **RANGE:** Widespread.

DIFFERENTIAL GRASSHOPPER
Melanoplus differentialis

Male Differential Grasshoppers, members of the short-horned grasshopper family, are known for their buzzing sounds and for destroying grass and crops. The sounds are made by rubbing the hind leg against the fore wing or by rubbing the wings together (when in flight). The insect's jumping power comes from muscles in the hind legs. Some short-horns are called locusts.

CAROLINA LOCUST
Dissosteira carolina

LOOK FOR: A grayish-brown color, this insect can easily blend in with the dry fields and grasses of its habitat. **LENGTH:** 1⅜–2". **HABITAT:** Grassy fields, open areas. **RANGE:** Widespread.

GREEN VALLEY GRASSHOPPER
Schistocerca shoshone

LOOK FOR: A large, green grasshopper with pink to reddish lower hind legs (not visible in photograph). **LENGTH:** 1½–2¾". **HABITAT:** Grasslands, open woods. **RANGE:** California and across the Southwest.

LOOK FOR: A shiny, golden-brown grasshopper with big compound eyes. The upper hind leg has a pattern of black V-shaped stripes.

LENGTH: 1¾".

HABITAT: Grassy plains, open woods.

RANGE: Widespread.

63

A lthough common, this katydid is not easy to spot against a backdrop of leafy branches. It is vocal, however, especially during the summer mating season. Then, male katydids chirp from the treetops, creating a din almost impossible to ignore, calling *katy-DID, katy-DID!*

LOOK FOR: Very bright green; the katydid's rounded, cross-veined wings look like leaves.

LENGTH: 2⅛".

HABITAT: Leafy forests.

RANGE: Eastern United States, southern Canada.

FORK-TAILED BUSH KATYDID
Scudderia furcata

LOOK FOR: Grass-green body, accented with brown. Relatively narrow wings extend beyond insect's abdomen.
LENGTH: 2". **HABITAT:** Forests, woods.
RANGE: Widespread.

CALIFORNIA KATYDID
Microcentrum californicum

LOOK FOR: Green, with leaf-shaped wings that taper toward the back.
LENGTH: 2⅜". **HABITAT:** Woodlands.
RANGE: California and across the Southwest.

65

FIELD CRICKET
Gryllus pennsylvanicus

The clear, high notes of the cricket's song can be heard from early spring to fall, day or night. In almost all species, it is the male that sings to attract a mate. When a female appears, the male dances around her, stroking her with his antennae. Every species has its own song, so each cricket can identify a member of its own species.

HOUSE CRICKET
Acheta domestica

LOOK FOR: Light brown body. When at rest, the hind wings extend beyond abdomen. Song is a triple chirp. **LENGTH:** ¾". **HABITAT:** Mostly indoors, in kitchens. **RANGE:** Widespread.

JERUSALEM CRICKET
Stenopelmatus fuscus

LOOK FOR: An amber-colored cricket with dark brown stripes. Large head, long antennae, no wings. **LENGTH:** 1⅛–2". **HABITAT:** Hillsides. **RANGE:** Plains, western regions.

SNOWY TREE CRICKET
Oecanthus fultoni

LOOK FOR: A light green cricket with broad, clear wings that lie flat on back. **LENGTH:** ⅞". **HABITAT:** Woods, gardens. **RANGE:** Widespread except Southeast.

LOOK FOR: A flat-backed, black to reddish-brown body with long antennae. Two antenna-like organs (cerci) extend from the rear.

LENGTH: ⅝–1".

HABITAT: Meadows, weeds.

RANGE: Widespread.

COMMON WATER STRIDER
Gerris remigis

Patrolling the surface of almost any pond or slow stream are Water Striders, the insects that literally walk on water. Also known as Pond Skaters, these bugs don't float but instead take advantage of water's surface tension.

LOOK FOR: A black, slender, spider-like body with extremely long middle and hind legs. The front legs are short and are used for grasping prey. These insects are usually wingless.

LENGTH: ⅜–1".

HABITAT: Surfaces of ponds, lakes, slow streams.

RANGE: Widespread.

WHIRLIGIG BEETLES
Family *Gyrinidae*

LOOK FOR: Black beetle with a seed-shaped body. Swims in circles on the water's surface. **LENGTH:** ⅜". **HABITAT:** Ponds, slow streams. **RANGE:** Throughout North America.

GIANT WATER BUG
Lethocerus americanus

LOOK FOR: Large, flat, dark body with greenish-brown wings; short beak. Also called Toe Biter. **LENGTH:** 2⅜". **HABITAT:** Ponds. **RANGE:** Widespread. **CAUTION:** Stings if disturbed.

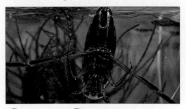

COMMON BACKSWIMMER
Notonecta undulata

LOOK FOR: Insect swimming on back, propelling itself by rowing with hind legs. **LENGTH:** ½". **HABITAT:** Ponds; slow, shallow streams. **RANGE:** Widespread. **CAUTION:** May sting.

GREEN STINK BUG
Acrosternum hilare

S tink bugs are aptly named: When threatened, they release a fluid with a disagreeable odor. The large stink glands are on the insect's underside. Stink bugs feed on the juices of leaves, flowers, and fruit trees, often causing much damage to crops.

LOOK FOR: All bright green except for narrow spots of yellow, orange, red, and black along sides and below. Head is small. Antennae have five segments.

LENGTH: ¾".

HABITAT: Orchards, gardens, crop fields.

RANGE: Widespread.

HARLEQUIN CABBAGE BUG
Murgantia histrionica

LOOK FOR: A shiny, black stink bug with orange-red markings on a smooth, shield-shaped back. Also called Calico Bug or Fire Bug. **LENGTH:** ⅜". **HABITAT:** Crops such as cabbage, broccoli, cauliflower; in orchards, gardens, meadows. **RANGE:** Widespread.

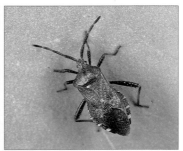

SQUASH BUG
Anasa tristis

LOOK FOR: Grayish-brown bug with orangish markings on abdomen. **LENGTH:** ⅝". **HABITAT:** Gardens, squash fields. **RANGE:** Widespread.

71

BLOOD-SUCKING CONENOSE
Triatoma sanguisuga

The Conenose lives in mattresses and other bedding, emerging at night to bite unsuspecting sleepers. Although it can fly, this bug stays on the ground once its belly is full.

Look for: A brownish-black bug with orange markings that make the bug look striped along its edges. Its narrow head extends beyond the eyes, ending in a rounded point.

Length: ¾".

Habitat: Beds, walls; nests of mammals such as wood rats.

Range: East of the Rockies.

Caution: Bites.

Wheel Bug
Arilus cristatus

Look for: A brownish bug with curving row of sharp, spiny "teeth" on top of thorax. **Length:** 1⅛". **Habitat:** Meadows, crop fields. **Range:** East of the Rockies. **Caution:** Stabs if disturbed.

Florida Leaf-footed Bug
Acanthocephala femorata

Look for: Broad, blackish body; red-tipped antennae; flattened hind legs. **Length:** ⅞". **Habitat:** Fields, meadows. **Range:** Florida; similar species widely found in East.

Bee Assassin
Apiomerus spp.

Look for: A red bug with black-brown markings or a brown bug with yellow marks; attacks bees and other insects. **Length:** ⅝". **Habitat:** Meadows, gardens. **Range:** Widespread; mostly in West.

SMALL MILKWEED BUG
Lygaeus kalmii

The Small Milkweed Bug feeds on the juices of ripening milkweed seeds. Predators that are poisoned by toxins in milkweed do well to avoid eating this bug, whose body itself is poisonous to them.

LOOK FOR: A black, oval-shaped body with a red X on the fore wings and a red band across the front of the thorax. Unlike similar insects in other families, this bug has both single eyes and compound eyes.

LENGTH: ⅜–½"

HABITAT: Meadows and fields with milkweed.

RANGE: Widespread.

BOXELDER BUG
Genus *Leptocoris*

LOOK FOR: A long, narrow, oval-shaped bug that is black to gray-brown with red markings. **LENGTH:** ⅝". **HABITAT:** Forests, gardens. **RANGE:** Widespread.

LARGE MILKWEED BUG
Oncopeltus fasciatus

LOOK FOR: A long, narrow, oval-shaped bug, black with orange-red pattern on back. **LENGTH:** ⅜–⅝". **HABITAT:** Milkweed fields. **RANGE:** East of the Rockies.

PERIODICAL CICADA
Magicicada spp.

These cicadas are unique in that they reach maturity together in huge broods. The nymphs develop slowly, over periods of 13 or 17 years, depending on the species. Then, within a few weeks, vast numbers of adult cicadas burst out of their nymphal skins. Their characteristic call, a buzz or whine, is so loud that it can cause damage to human ears.

LOOK FOR: A black body with clear, orange-veined wings; large, prominent red eyes; reddish legs.

LENGTH: 1⅛".

HABITAT: Woodlands, grasslands, fields.

RANGE: Eastern United States.

GRAND WESTERN CICADA
Tibicen dorsata

LOOK FOR: A brown or greenish cicada with veined wings. Outspread wings measure 4½" from tip to tip. **LENGTH:** 1⅜". **HABITAT:** Forests. **RANGE:** Colorado and the southwestern United States.

DOGDAY HARVESTFLY
Tibicen canicularis

LOOK FOR: A black-and-green cicada with transparent green fore wings. Call is an intense buzzing sound. **LENGTH:** 1¼". **HABITAT:** Forests. **RANGE:** North-eastern United States and southern Canada.

77

SHARPSHOOTER
Oncometopia nigricans

LOOK FOR: A tube-shaped, yellow-orange treehopper with black markings; black dots on front of yellow pronotum (upper thorax). The name comes from the insect's ability to "shoot" tiny liquid drops from the tip of its abdomen.
LENGTH: ⅜". **HABITAT:** Meadows, open lands. **RANGE:** Florida.

OAK TREEHOPPER
Platycotis vittata

LOOK FOR: A thorn-shaped insect, light blue with red striping or olive to greenish-bronze. Bumpy texture helps it to look like an inedible part of the plant. **LENGTH:** ⅜". **HABITAT:** Oak forests. **RANGE:** Northwest, West, Southwest.

The Scarlet-and-green Leafhopper is a common sight in grass, feeding on plant juices and hopping from plant to plant. Young leafhoppers run sideways; adults (tiny though they are) can fly a distance of 150 miles, aided by wind.

LOOK FOR: This beautiful leafhopper is a brilliant green to blue-green, with lengthwise bands of orange-red on wings.

LENGTH: ⅜".

HABITAT: Grassy meadows, gardens.

RANGE: Eastern North America.

79

GREEN APPLE APHID
Aphis pomi

The Green Apple Aphid can cause great damage to fruit trees. With its special beak-like projection, this bug sucks out the sap of a tree, eventually killing it. Though tiny, these insects are so numerous that they are considered serious pests.

LOOK FOR: Masses of tiny green or yellowish insects on a plant. Each aphid has a soft, pear-shaped body and dark legs.

LENGTH: 1/16–1/8".

HABITAT: Orchards.

RANGE: Widespread.

Cottony Cushion Scale
Icerya purchasi

Look for: Female is reddish, with white, furrowed egg sac attached to the end of her body. **Length:** ¼". **Habitat:** Woods, orchards, grass. **Range:** Southern half of United States.

Common Thrips
Family *Thripidae*

Look for: A tiny insect—a speck of yellow, brown, black, or yellow and orange with narrow, pointed wings. **Length:** ⅟₆₀". **Habitat:** Fields, gardens. **Range:** Widespread.

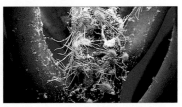

Long-tailed Mealybug
Pseudococcus adonidum

Look for: A tiny, white insect with one to five threadlike tails; shorter threads on sides. **Length:** ⅟₆₀–⅛". **Habitat:** Outdoor plants in South; indoors in North. **Range:** Widespread.

81

EASTERN DOBSONFLY
Corydalus cornutus

The male Eastern Dobsonfly's mandibles (jaws) look like long tusks. They are used to clasp the female while mating. Adult dobsonflies live only a few days. The larvae may live two to three years, provided they do not first become a meal for a fish.

LOOK FOR: Long, slender body and long, transparent, grayish wings with dark veins. Wingspan is almost five inches. Female's mandibles are short and strong, quite useful for self-defense.

LENGTH: 2".

HABITAT: On woody plants near fast-flowing streams and rivers.

RANGE: East of the Rockies.

CAUTION: Bites.

LARGE CADDISFLY
Family *Phryganeidae*

LOOK FOR: Brownish wings with dark mottling. Larvae build movable tube-shaped shelters from bits of plants. **LENGTH:** ½–1". **HABITAT:** Ponds, marshes. **RANGE:** Widespread.

ALDERFLY
Sialis spp.

LOOK FOR: A black-to-brown insect smaller than dobsonfly or caddisfly. Wings are brown-tinged. **LENGTH:** ⅜". **HABITAT:** Near streams. **RANGE:** Northern North America.

GREEN LACEWING
Chrysopa spp.

LOOK FOR: Four oval, pale green, veined wings. The bulging eyes are metallic yellow. Lacewings release a foul smell when touched. **LENGTH:** ⅜". **HABITAT:** Woods, fields. **RANGE:** Widespread.

83

SIX-SPOTTED GREEN TIGER BEETLE
Cicindela sexguttata

Unlike many other beetles, tiger beetles are active in broad daylight and are fast runners and fliers. The brilliant iridescent green color of this particular tiger beetle helps identify it.

LOOK FOR: An iridescent green beetle with long, thin legs and long antennae. Fore wings sometimes have six or more large white spots along the rear edge.

LENGTH: ⅝".

HABITAT: Paths and sunny areas in forests.

RANGE: East of the Rockies.

BEAUTIFUL TIGER BEETLE
Cicindela formosa

LOOK FOR: A beetle with bright metallic colors, long hairy legs, and long jaws It is a fast runner and flier. **LENGTH:** ¾".
HABITAT: Beaches, lakeshores, deserts, woods **RANGE:** Throughout North America. **CAUTION:** Bites.

CATERPILLAR HUNTER
Calosoma spp.

LOOK FOR: An oval beetle with grooved, green fore wings, edged with coppery gold. One species of this beetle was introduced from Eurasia to eat the destructive Gypsy Moth caterpillar.
LENGTH: 1–1⅜". **HABITAT:** Woods, gardens.
RANGE: Widespread.

85

COMMON BLACK GROUND BEETLE
Pterostichus spp.

The Common Black Ground Beetle hides under rocks and logs in the daytime, then crawls out after dark in search of soft insects to eat. Ground beetles are fast runners, a valuable trait for hunting.

LOOK FOR: A glossy black beetle with small, tapered head, large eyes, and prominent jaws. Hard fore wings are evenly grooved.

LENGTH: ½–⅝".

HABITAT: Under stones and logs in moist places.

RANGE: Widespread.

TUMBLEBUG
Canthon spp.

LOOK FOR: A black beetle, sometimes with a tinge of color. This beetle recycles mammals' dung by shaping it into a ball and rolling it into a hole— the female then lays a single egg on it. **LENGTH:** ⅜–¾". **HABITAT:** Fields, pastures. **RANGE:** Widespread.

YELLOW MEALWORM BEETLE
Tenebrio molitor

LOOK FOR: Black to reddish-black, lozenge-shaped body with rounded head and "corners" on upper thorax. **LENGTH:** ½–⅝". **HABITAT:** Storage areas for cereals and grain. **RANGE:** Widespread.

87

ELEPHANT STAG BEETLE
Lucanus elephus

Male stag beetles use their awesome mandibles (jaws) to flip over other males when fighting over females. Once overturned, these large beetles must struggle to get themselves right side up. They are also called "pinching bugs."

LOOK FOR: A flat, shiny, reddish-brown body with antler-like mandibles. The male's mandibles are one-half inch long; the female's are smaller.

LENGTH: 1¾–2⅜".

HABITAT: Woods.

RANGE: Virginia and North Carolina, west to Oklahoma, northeast to Illinois.

RUGOSE STAG BEETLE
Sinodendron rugosum

LOOK FOR: Short, curved horn extending from head; head narrower than thorax. The larvae of these beetles enrich the soil as they recycle dead trees: They feed on the wood and deposit their waste matter in the soil. **LENGTH:** ¾". **HABITAT:** Woods. **RANGE:** West Coast.

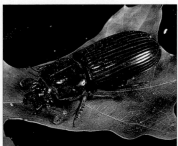

PATENT-LEATHER BEETLE
Odontotaenius disjunctus

LOOK FOR: A shiny, black beetle with long, flattened body; short horn extending from head; antennae bent. **LENGTH:** 1⅝". **HABITAT:** Woods, forests. **RANGE:** Eastern United States and parts of Canada.

89

JAPANESE BEETLE
Popilla japonica

Since its discovery in New Jersey in 1916, the imported Japanese Beetle has spread across the northeastern United States, destroying gardens, lawns, and golf courses along the way. This beetle damages more than 200 plant species. The larvae attack the roots of grasses, and the adults feed on the leaves, flowers, and fruits of cultivated plants.

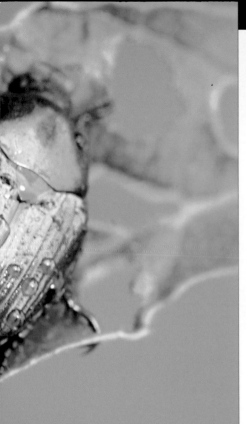

MAY BEETLE (JUNE BUG)
Phyllophaga spp.

LOOK FOR: A glossy, reddish-brown beetle; antennae bent at right angles at tips; makes a buzzing sound. **LENGTH:** ¾–1⅜". **HABITAT:** Forests, grasslands, suburbs. **RANGE:** Widespread.

TEN-LINED JUNE BEETLE
Polyphylla decimlineata

LOOK FOR: A brown beetle with long white stripes. **LENGTH:** 1–1⅜". **HABITAT:** Forests. **RANGE:** Rocky Mountain states, Southwest.

DOGBANE LEAF BEETLE
Chrysochus auratus

LOOK FOR: An oblong, green beetle, often with brassy fore wings; produces an unpleasant odor when threatened. **LENGTH:** ¼". **HABITAT:** Fields, roadsides. **RANGE:** Eastern North America.

LOOK FOR: Adults have a rounded, oval, metallic green body with brownish or red-orange fore wings. Abdomen is ringed with white hair tufts.

LENGTH: ⅜–½".

HABITAT: Gardens, yards, woods.

RANGE: Maine to South Carolina, west to Ohio.

91

FIREFLY
Family *Lampyridae*

Also called lightning bugs, Fireflies are neither bugs nor flies: They are beetles. Fireflies use their light-producing organs to flash each other coded messages, all in the interest of finding a mate. The male signals as he flies; the female answers from her hiding place. Each species flashes its own special pattern.

LOOK FOR: A long, dark, soft-bodied beetle with flashing "tail" light at the tip of the abdomen. Wing covers are blackish, edged in yellow.

LENGTH: ¼–¾".

HABITAT: Meadows, woods, backyards, gardens.

RANGE: Widespread in eastern United States and southern Canada.

AMERICAN CARRION BEETLE
Silpha americana
LOOK FOR: A large black beetle with upper part of thorax ivory to yellow with black center; raised ridges on fore wings.
LENGTH: ⅜–⅞". **HABITAT:** Dead, decaying animals. **RANGE:** East of the Rockies.

FIRE BEETLE
Dendroides spp.
LOOK FOR: Head and upper thorax are orangish (fore wings can be black). Male: antennae are branched. **LENGTH:** ⅜–½".
HABITAT: Woods. **RANGE:** Widespread.

BANDED NET-WING
Calopteron reticulatum
LOOK FOR: Brownish fore wings with black horizontal bands. **LENGTH:** ⅜–¾". **HABITAT:** Fields, woods, meadows. **RANGE:** Eastern United States, southern Canada.

Two-spotted Ladybug Beetle

Adalia bipunctata

One of the best places to find ladybug beetles is on a plant that is infested with aphids. By devouring these sap-sucking pests, the adult beetle and its black larvae help to protect the host plant. The number of spots a ladybug has depends on the species, not the insect's age. Some ladybugs have no spots at all—still others are striped.

LOOK FOR: Reddish-orange fore wings with one large black spot on each. Head and thorax jet-black with light-colored markings.

LENGTH: ⅛–¼".

HABITAT: Meadows, fields, forests, gardens, houses.

RANGE: Widespread.

RED MILKWEED BEETLE
Tetraopes tetraophthalmus

LOOK FOR: Four black spots on upper thorax and a variety of different patterns of black dots and streaks on red fore wings. Long, tubular body.
LENGTH: ⅜–½". **HABITAT:** Meadows and fields with milkweed. **RANGE:** Eastern North America.

CONVERGENT LADYBUG BEETLE
Hippodamia convergens

LOOK FOR: Thirteen black spots on reddish-orange fore wings; two white stripes that come together on black upper thorax. Oval body. **LENGTH:** ⅛".
HABITAT: Woods, meadows, gardens.
RANGE: Widespread.

95

LOCUST BORER
Megacyllene robiniae

LONG-JAWED LONGHORN
Dendrobius mandibularis

LOOK FOR: Long, black, oval-shaped body with two yellow bands on fore wings divided by black along the midline. Black-and-yellow antennae look striped; the male's are longer than its body. **LENGTH:** ¾–1¼".
HABITAT: Forests. **RANGE:** Southwest.

PENNSYLVANIA LEATHER-WING
Chauliognathus pennsylvanicus

LOOK FOR: Long, brownish-yellow body with a large, black oval spot on rear of each wing. Also a short black band across thorax. **LENGTH:** ⅜–½". **HABITAT:** Gardens and fields. **RANGE:** Eastern and central United States.

L ocust Borers are so-named because the larvae bore tunnels into the trunks of black locust trees. The young beetles grow and develop underneath the bark, feeding on the soft, outer wood. The tree cannot grow properly and may not survive as a result of these pests.

LOOK FOR: A long, thin, black body with yellow stripes on head and thorax, forming Ws down the middle of the body. Legs are dark red. The male's antennae are almost as long as its body.

LENGTH: ½–¾".

HABITAT: Woods that include black locust trees.

RANGE: Eastern United States and Canada.

BOLL WEEVIL
Anthonomus grandis

STORED-GRAIN BILLBUG
(GRANARY WEEVIL) *Silophilus granarius*

LOOK FOR: A glossy, dark brown body, with pitted thorax and deeply grooved wing covers. Thick beak and oval club at the end of each antenna; no flying wings. **LENGTH:** ⅛". **HABITAT:** Where grain is grown or stored. **RANGE:** Widespread.

The dreaded Boll Weevil, a mere quarter of an inch long, can destroy most of the bolls (seedpods) in a cotton field, causing the crop to fail. The female lays a single egg in each boll, up to a total of 300. The larvae feed on the bolls from the inside, as the adults eat them from the outside.

LOOK FOR: A gray-black to brown, hard-bodied beetle that is covered with light-colored, furry-textured scales. Curved, snout-like beak is longer in female than male. Wing covers have thin, lengthwise grooves.

LENGTH: ⅙–¼".

HABITAT: Cotton fields.

RANGE: The South to California.

ROSE WEEVIL
Rhynchites bicolor

LOOK FOR: A mostly red weevil with a long, thick, black beak. **LENGTH:** ¼".
HABITAT: Fields and gardens with bushes of rose, blackberry, and raspberry.
RANGE: Widespread.

99

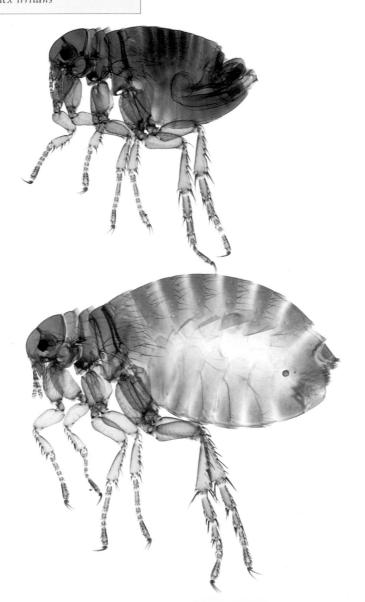

Fleas are named after the type of animal they usually live on (for example, Dog Flea or Human Flea), although they can switch from one type of animal to another. The Human Flea will suck blood daily from its host; however, it can live without food for several months. It helped to spread the bubonic plague—a deadly disease that killed about 75 million people in Europe in the 14th century (25–50 percent of the population at that time).

LOOK FOR: A tiny, pale or dark insect—a speck—with very flattened sides. Tip of male's body curves upward; female's curves downward.

LENGTH: $\frac{1}{16}$".

HABITAT: Adult fleas live in hair and clothing. Larvae are found under rugs and inside the contents of vacuum cleaners.

RANGE: Widespread.

CAUTION: Bites.

SNOW FLEA
Achorutes nivicola

LOOK FOR: Dark blue, cigar-shaped body; swarms in masses above snow cover. **LENGTH:** $\frac{1}{16}$". **HABITAT:** Forest floor. **RANGE:** East Coast to Pennsylvania, west to Iowa, north to the Arctic.

SEASHORE SPRINGTAIL
Anurida maritima

LOOK FOR: A tiny gray insect with no wings; a two-prong springing organ on underside releases a catch, popping the insect upward. **LENGTH:** $\frac{1}{8}$". **HABITAT:** Beaches. **RANGE:** Widespread.

HUMAN BODY LOUSE
(COOTIE) *Pediculus humanus*

LOOK FOR: Tiny gray-brown insect with a narrow head. **LENGTH:** $\frac{1}{8}$". **HABITAT:** Human bodies; clothing and bedding. **RANGE:** Widespread.

101

C rane Flies look a bit like oversized, long-legged mosquitoes, but they do not bite. In fact, the adult Crane Fly does not eat at all, although it may end up as food for a bird or bat. It does all its eating in the larval stage, during which time it feeds on plant roots and other vegetation.

GIANT WESTERN CRANE FLY
Holorusia rubiginosa

LOOK FOR: Greenish-brown insect with reddish abdomen, olive tinged wings, and long legs. **LENGTH:** 1⅜". **HABITAT:** Moist areas: muddy woods and edges of streams. **RANGE:** West Coast, Pacific Northwest.

PHANTOM CRANE FLY
Bittacomorpha clavipes

LOOK FOR: A needle-thin, black body with long, spidery legs, banded in white. Clear wings with fine black veins. **LENGTH:** ½". **HABITAT:** Humid areas along the edges of streams. **RANGE:** Eastern United States and Canada.

LOOK FOR: Slender, brown body; clear, veined wings; and long, thin legs that break off easily. The abdomen is longer than the head and thorax combined.
LENGTH: ⅜–2½".

HABITAT: Wet or muddy ground; may enter houses.

RANGE: Widespread.

103

HOUSE MOSQUITO
Culex pipiens

The male House Mosquito feeds on nectar and other plant juices. It is the female that sucks blood from birds, reptiles, people, and other mammals. She needs the protein in the blood for her eggs.

LOOK FOR: Long, slender, soft body with light brown thorax; one pair of narrow wings; and long, thin, brown "beak," or proboscis. The male's antennae are more feathery than the female's.

LENGTH: ⅛–¼".

HABITAT: Near swamps, ponds, and other bodies of stagnant water.

RANGE: Widespread.

CAUTION: Bites.

MALARIA-CARRYING MOSQUITO
Anopheles spp.

LOOK FOR: A dark brown body. When it lands, it stands on its head. **LENGTH:** ⅛".
HABITAT: Forests. **RANGE:** Widespread.
CAUTION: Bites.

COMMON MIDGE
Chironomus attenuatus

LOOK FOR: Mosquito-like insect with pale green or brown body, pale bown wings. Lacks "beak." **LENGTH:** ¼". **HABITAT:** Near water. **RANGE:** Widespread.

BLACK FLY
Simulium spp.

LOOK FOR: A grayish-brown to shiny black fly, with short antennae and smoky wings. **LENGTH:** 1/16–⅛". **HABITAT:** Near streams in forests. **RANGE:** Widespread except Florida. **CAUTION:** Bites.

AMERICAN HORSE FLY
Tabanus americanus

This fly was named after the female of the species, which feeds on the blood of large animals such as horses. Silent in motion, the female lands on its prey unnoticed, delivering a painful bite with knife-like mouthparts. The male horse fly eats pollen and nectar.

LOOK FOR: A very large, hairy, brown-black body with dark wings and large, green, bulging eyes; reddish antennae and legs.

LENGTH: ¾–1⅛".

HABITAT: Swamps, marshes, ponds, farms.

RANGE: Widespread except Far West.

CAUTION: Bites.

DEER FLY
Chrysops spp.

LOOK FOR: Yellow-green markings on a black, flattened body; head somewhat smaller than a horse fly's; green or gold eyes; a brown-black pattern on wings. **LENGTH:** ⅜–⅝". **HABITAT:** Forests, meadows, roadsides, suburbs. **RANGE:** Widespread. **CAUTION:** Bites.

BLACK HORSE FLY
Tabanus atratus

LOOK FOR: A black body with yellowish or black hair on thorax; abdomen has bluish sheen; unlike Deer Fly, wings are not patterned. **LENGTH:** ¾–1⅛". **HABITAT:** Meadows, grasslands, marshes, slow streams. **RANGE:** Widespread. **CAUTION:** Bites.

107

ROBBER FLY
Family *Asilidae*

A Robber Fly attacks an insect in the air by capturing it with its spiny legs, then stabbing it with its sharp beak. Then the Robber Fly drinks the juices of its prey.

LOOK FOR: A gray, usually slender fly with spiny legs and black markings on thorax and abdomen.

Has "bearded" face and three simple eyes. Some species sound like bumblebees.

LENGTH: ¼–1⅛".

HABITAT: Fields, woods, gardens.

RANGE: East of the Rockies.

CAUTION: Bites if touched.

FLOWER-LOVING FLY
Apiocera haruspex

LOOK FOR: A tan or gray fly with dark markings similar to robber fly but without bristles. Eats flower nectar, not insects. **LENGTH:** ⅛–¼". **HABITAT:** Deserts, gardens, pastures. **RANGE:** West.

BEE KILLER
Promachus fitchii

LOOK FOR: Long, brown body; silvery hair at tip of abdomen; eats bees and wasps. **LENGTH:** ¼–1⅛". **HABITAT:** Meadows, fields. **RANGE:** East of the Rockies.

HOUSE FLY
Musca domestica

House Flies are hard to swat because they react to movement five times faster than humans do. Sensitive hairs on their bodies send data directly to the wings, so these flies can take off the instant motion is detected. In humans, the sensory data must usually first be processed by the brain. Female House Flies live for about 26 days; males, about 15 days.

LOOK FOR: A gray body with black stripes along the thorax; hairy legs with adhesive pads on the feet; antennae with a feathery bristle; large, reddish-brown eyes; and mouthparts adapted for lapping up food.

LENGTH: ⅛–¼".

HABITAT: In or near houses and farms.

RANGE: Widespread.

TACHINID FLY
Family *Tachinidae*

LOOK FOR: Similar to House Fly; many are larger and/or hairier. **LENGTH:** ⅛–½". **HABITAT:** Fields, meadows. **RANGE:** Widespread.

BLUE BOTTLE FLY
Calliphora vomitoria

LOOK FOR: Gray head, red eyes, dark gray thorax, and metallic blue abdomen. **LENGTH:** ½". **HABITAT:** Pastures, barnyards. **RANGE:** Widespread.

BITING STABLE FLY
Stomoxys calcitrans

LOOK FOR: Gray body with four dark stripes on thorax. Mouthparts point forward for biting. **LENGTH:** ¼–⅜". **HABITAT:** Coasts, farms, garbage dumps. **RANGE:** Widespread. **CAUTION:** Bites.

111

EASTERN TIGER SWALLOWTAIL
Papilio glaucus

Swallowtails are large, eye-catching butterflies with long tails that resemble the forked tail feathers of swallows. Brightly striped or spotted with highly contrasting colors, these butterflies are among the easiest to spot in the eastern United States.

LOOK FOR: Yellow wings with black stripes; long, black tail on each hind wing; and yellow-spotted black band along rear edges of wings. Some females have dark wings with yellow-and-blue spots near the edge.

WINGSPAN: 3⅛–5⅞".

HABITAT: Forests, meadows, parks, suburbs, gardens.

RANGE: East of the Rockies.

ANISE SWALLOWTAIL
Papilio zelicaon

LOOK FOR: Black wings with big yellow spots; hind wings have blue spots and orange eyespots. **WINGSPAN:** 2⅝–3½".
HABITAT: All habitats except dense forests.
RANGE: West.

BLACK SWALLOWTAIL
Papilio polyxenes

LOOK FOR: Black wings with a double row of spots on fore wings; orange eyespots on hind wings. **WINGSPAN:** 2⅝–3½". **HABITAT:** Meadows, parks. **RANGE:** East of the Rockies.

ZEBRA SWALLOWTAIL
Eurytides marcellus

LOOK FOR: Long tails; greenish-white wings with black stripes; hind wings have red and blue spots above tails. **WINGSPAN:** 2½–4½". **HABITAT:** Wooded streams, marshes, swamps. **RANGE:** East.

113

CABBAGE WHITE
Pieris rapae

Can you guess what the caterpillars of this butterfly like to eat? If you used the butterfly's name as a clue, you are right! The caterpillars have a taste for cabbages—as well as radishes and nasturtium flowers. As a result, farmers and gardeners consider this butterfly a nuisance.

Look for: Yellowish white hind wings and white fore wings with gray tips. The male has one black spot on each fore wing; the female has two. The caterpillar is bright green with yellow stripes.

Wingspan: 1¼–1⅞".

Habitat: Gardens, farms, fields, cities.

Range: Widespread except most northerly regions.

CLOUDED SULPHUR
Colias philodice

Look for: Yellow fore wings. Male: black border on fore wings. Female: yellow-and-black border. **Wingspan:** 1⅜–2". **Habitat:** Fields, meadows, parks. **Range:** Widespread except Southwest, Florida.

MUSTARD WHITE
Pieris napi

Look for: Rounded wings; white above and veined; cream to yellowish below. Also known as Veined White. **Wingspan:** 1½–1⅝". **Habitat:** Woods. **Range:** Widespread except Southeast.

SARA ORANGETIP
Anthocharis sara

Look for: Wings white above, black-bordered, orange band on fore wing of male; female varies. **Wingspan:** 1⅝". **Habitat:** Mountains, coastal plains, deserts. **Range:** Western United States.

115

SPRING AZURE
Celastrina ladon

Most species of blue butterflies are found in the West, but the Spring Azure is widespread. It is usually seen in the spring and early summer.

LOOK FOR: Wings bluish above, gray with darker gray spots below. The female has a coal-black border on the fore wing.

WINGSPAN: ¾–1¼".

HABITAT: Woods, fields, wetlands.

RANGE: Widespread except parts of Florida, Louisiana, and Texas.

GRAY HAIRSTREAK
Strymon melinus

LOOK FOR: Orange spot on hind wings near the shorter of two blackish tails. Wings above are grayish-brown; pale gray below with thin black-and-white bands. **WINGSPAN:** 1¼". **HABITAT:** Meadows, roadsides, crop fields. **RANGE:** Widespread.

AMERICAN COPPER
Lycaena phlaeas

LOOK FOR: Fore wings are bright orange with dark spots and dark border. Hind wings have a red-orange band near the edge on the underside. **WINGSPAN:** ⅞–1⅛". **HABITAT:** Meadows, fields, roadsides; alpine areas. **RANGE:** Widespread; more common in the East.

117

Monarchs are amazing fliers and navigators. Every autumn, millions of them migrate from eastern and central North America south to Mexico and begin the journey back north in the spring: a round trip of thousands of miles! In spring, females lay eggs on their way back north, and their newly hatched offspring complete the trip for them.

VICEROY
Limenitis archippus

LOOK FOR: Wings similar to the Monarch, but somewhat smaller and darker with a crosswise black line on each wing. **WINGSPAN:** 3". **HABITAT:** Meadows, fields, wetlands. **RANGE:** Widespread.

RED ADMIRAL
Vanessa atalanta

LOOK FOR: Dark brown fore wings with white spots and wide orange bands. **WINGSPAN:** 1¼–2⅜". **HABITAT:** Woods, meadows, gardens. **RANGE:** Widespread except far north.

MOURNING CLOAK
Nymphalis antiopa

LOOK FOR: Purplish-brown wings; black band with blue spots is edged with yellow. **WINGSPAN:** 3⅜". **HABITAT:** Woods, streamsides, gardens. **RANGE:** Widespread except far north; rare in Deep South.

LOOK FOR: Large, brown-orange wings with black veins and thick black outlines, which are dotted with white. Caterpillar feeds on milkweed, causing adult butterfly to taste bad to most birds.

WINGSPAN: 3½–4".

HABITAT: Fields, roadsides, and other areas where milkweed grows.

RANGE: Widespread except far north.

119

SILVER-SPOTTED SKIPPER
Epargyreus clarus

Skippers have narrow, sharply angled wings that enable them to fly from place to place in short skips. The Silver-spotted Skipper is commonly seen throughout most of North America, especially in areas where people live.

LOOK FOR: Brown fore wings with yellow-orange spots above; hind wings have a large silver patch below. The two-inch caterpillar is yellowish to green with dark spots and a reddish head.

WINGSPAN: 1¾–2⅜".
HABITAT: Suburbs, fields, hillsides, gardens.
RANGE: Widespread.

FIERY SKIPPER
Hylephila phyleus

LOOK FOR: Yellowish-orange to brown on wings; pale orange with black dots below. **WINGSPAN:** 1¼". **HABITAT:** Lawns, parks, fields. **RANGE:** Widespread.

COMMON CHECKERED SKIPPER
Pyrgus communis

LOOK FOR: Often black with pattern of white spots, but this can vary. **WINGSPAN:** ¾–1¼". **HABITAT:** Meadows, deserts. **RANGE:** Widespread except northern states.

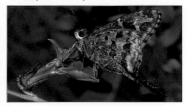

LONG-TAILED SKIPPER
Urbanus proteus

LOOK FOR: Long tail; chunky, iridescent blue-green body; fore wings brown-gray below. **WINGSPAN:** 1½–2". **HABITAT:** Fields, roadsides, shores. **RANGE:** Southeast to southern California.

121

INDIAN MEAL MOTH
Plodia interpunctella

Indian meal is a term for cornmeal, which is what these major pests eat, along with other starchy foods such as packaged cereals and dried fruit.

CLOTHES MOTH
Family *Tineidae*

LOOK FOR: Small moth. Wings are pale, silvery gray. **WINGSPAN:** ⅛–1⅛". **HABITAT:** Fungus, vegetables, woolens. **RANGE:** Widespread.

MILL MOTH
Ephestia kuehniella

LOOK FOR: Gray body and fore wings. Wings crossed by dark zigzags. **WINGSPAN:** ⅞". **HABITAT:** Flour mills, grain bins. **RANGE:** Widespread.

LOOK FOR: Fore wings are mostly coppery brown, grayish beige near body.

WINGSPAN: ⅝".

HABITAT: Pantries and other places where dry foods are stored.

RANGE: Widespread.

MEXICAN JUMPING BEAN
MOTH (LARVAL STAGE)
Carpocapsa saltitans

LOOK FOR: The caterpillar of this species lives inside a seed, which it eats. When the caterpillar jerks its body, the seed jumps. **HABITAT:** Desert. **RANGE:** Southwest.

123

LUNA MOTH
Actias luna

CECROPIA MOTH
Hyalophora cecropia

LOOK FOR: Dark wings with red-and-white crossbands, white crescents, and eyespots. **WINGSPAN:** 4¾–5⅞". **HABITAT:** Forests, suburbs, cities. **RANGE:** East of the Rockies.

IMPERIAL MOTH
Eacles imperialis

LOOK FOR: Mustard-colored wings with patches of dusty rose. **WINGSPAN:** 4–5⅞". **HABITAT:** Forests. **RANGE:** East of the Rockies.

POLYPHEMUS MOTH
Antheraea polyphemus

LOOK FOR: Brownish-yellow wings with eyespots and a wavy black-and-white line near outer border. **WINGSPAN:** 3½–5½". **HABITAT:** Leafy forests. **RANGE:** East of the Rockies.

This moth, named after Luna, the Roman goddess of the moon, is one of the most spectacular-looking moths, with sweeping tails and feathery antennae. Unfortunately, it is threatened by the use of pesticides.

LOOK FOR: Pale green wings edged in front with purple and an eyespot on each wing; the hind wings have long, curved tails. The plump and hairy caterpillar (3⅛") is green with yellow stripes and red dots.

WINGSPAN: 3½–4½".

HABITAT: Leafy forests.

RANGE: Eastern United States, southern Canada.

HUMMINGBIRD MOTH
Hemaris thysbe

WHITE-LINED SPHINX
Hyles lineata

LOOK FOR: Brown fore wings with criss-crossed tan-and-white bands. **WINGSPAN:** 2½–3½". **HABITAT:** Deserts, meadows, roadsides, gardens. **RANGE:** Widespread.

TOMATO HORNWORM MOTH
Manduca quinquemaculata

LOOK FOR: Narrow, gray-brown wings; large, tapered body with five pairs of yellow spots. **WINGSPAN:** 4". **HABITAT:** Gardens. **RANGE:** Eastern North America.

BUMBLEBEE MOTH
Hemaris diffinus

LOOK FOR: A day-flying, fuzzy-bodied moth that looks like a bee. **WINGSPAN:** 1½–2". **HABITAT:** Forests, mountains, meadows, gardens. **RANGE:** Widespread.

Just like a hummingbird, this moth feeds by day, hovering in front of flowers, and drinking nectar with a long, flexible tube (proboscis). The proboscis rolls up when not in use.

LOOK FOR: A spindle-shaped body with bands of green, orange, and red across abdomen.

WINGSPAN: 1½–2".

HABITAT: Forests, rivers.

RANGE: Northern regions and the eastern United States.

127

GYPSY MOTH
Lymantria dispar

Brought to New England in 1869, the Gypsy Moth has proved to be a pest. The female lays many eggs on tree trunks. After the caterpillars (larvae) hatch from the eggs, they begin eating leaves, sometimes stripping a whole forest in one season. If you listen carefully, you can hear the caterpillars' waste pellets (frass) dropping!

LOOK FOR: A gray, hairy caterpillar with five pairs of blue bumps and then six pairs of red bumps on its back. The female moth has white wings with dark spots; the male's wings are speckled brown.

SIZE: Female wingspan 2¾"; male wingspan ⅛–1⅝"; caterpillar up to 2".

HABITAT: Forests.

RANGE: East to Midwest.

ORNATE TIGER MOTH
Apantesis ornata

LOOK FOR: Ivory-and-black "stained-glass" pattern on fore wings. Pinkish hind wings have black spots. **WINGSPAN:** 1⅛–1⅝". **HABITAT:** Roadsides, fields. **RANGE:** Great Basin to Pacific Coast.

EASTERN TENT CATERPILLAR MOTH
Malacosoma americana

LOOK FOR: Brown, hairy fore wings with two white lines. **WINGSPAN:** ⅞–1½". **HABITAT:** Leafy trees. **RANGE:** East.

WOOLLY BEAR CATERPILLAR MOTH
Isia isabella

LOOK FOR: Yellow-brown fore wings with black dots. Caterpillar: bristly, black and reddish. **WINGSPAN:** 1⅝–2". **HABITAT:** Meadows. **RANGE:** Widespread.

If you try to find a Sweetheart Underwing moth while it's resting on a tree trunk, you'll have to look very closely. Its grayish-brown fore wings seem to blend right into the tree's bark. If touched, however, the moth flashes the bold colors of its hind wings, startling any predator while the moth makes its getaway.

LOOK FOR: Speckled, grayish-brown fore wings; hind wings banded in orange, black, and pink, with white edging. The gray caterpillar looks like a twig.

WINGSPAN: 3–3⅜".

HABITAT: Forests, gardens.

RANGE: Widespread except West Coast.

ARMYWORM MOTH
Pseudalatia unipunctata

LOOK FOR: Brownish-gray with white spot near center of fore wing; hind wings lighter brown with darker scales along wing veins. **WINGSPAN:** 1½". **HABITAT:** Cultivated fields, grassy meadows, gardens. **RANGE:** Canada to Gulf states, east of the Rockies; also southwestern states.

TULIP TREE BEAUTY
Epimecis hortaria

LOOK FOR: A gray-brown moth with wavy brown crosslines on fore wings; hind wings similar. Rests on tree trunks with wings spread out. **WINGSPAN:** 1½–2". **HABITAT:** Moist forests. **RANGE:** Southern Canada to Florida; more common in the Appalachians and the South.

YELLOW JACKET
Vespula spp.

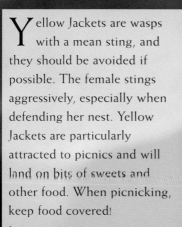

Yellow Jackets are wasps with a mean sting, and they should be avoided if possible. The female stings aggressively, especially when defending her nest. Yellow Jackets are particularly attracted to picnics and will land on bits of sweets and other food. When picnicking, keep food covered!

LOOK FOR: A stout body boldly banded with yellow (or white) and black; abdomen slim where it attaches to the thorax, creating a "waist" (pedicel). Wings are dark. **LENGTH:** ⅝". **HABITAT:** Meadows, forests, urban and suburban areas. **RANGE:** Widespread. **CAUTION:** Painful sting.

PAPER WASP
Polistes spp.

LOOK FOR: Slender, reddish-brown to black body with yellow stripes. **LENGTH:** ½–1". **HABITAT:** Meadows, fields, gardens, buildings. **RANGE:** Widespread. **CAUTION:** Stings.

BALD-FACED HORNET
Vespula maculata

LOOK FOR: Black-and-white pattern on body; dark wings; "waist" (pedicel) pinched in. **LENGTH:** ¾". **HABITAT:** Meadows, forests, houses, barns. **RANGE:** Widespread. **CAUTION:** Painful sting.

ICHNEUMON WASP
Family *Ichneumonidae*

LOOK FOR: A thin, long-legged wasp. The hoop-like structure is the female's organ for laying eggs. Most don't sting. **LENGTH:** ⅛–3". **HABITAT:** Forests. **RANGE:** Widespread except deserts and plains.

133

LITTLE BLACK ANT
Monomorium minimum

SIMILAR SPECIES

FIRE ANT
Solenopsis geminata

LOOK FOR: A yellow, red, or black ant with large head and a two-segmented "waist." **LENGTH:** ⅟₁₆–¼". **HABITAT:** Fields, woods. **RANGE:** Southern states to West Coast, north to Canada. **CAUTION:** Painful bite.

BLACK CARPENTER ANT
Camponotus pennsylvanicus

LOOK FOR: Black body, "waist" with one segment, gray hairs on abdomen. Twice as big as the Little Black Ant. **LENGTH:** ¼–½". **HABITAT:** Dead wood. **RANGE:** East of the Rockies.

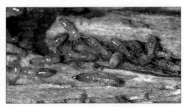

SUBTERRANEAN TERMITE
Reticulitermes flavipes

LOOK FOR: A small, soft-bodied insect; no ant-like "waist"; winged adults are black to brown; workers are light gray and eyeless. **LENGTH:** ¼". **HABITAT:** Soil, woods, moist wood. **RANGE:** East.

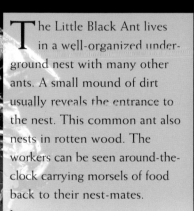

The Little Black Ant lives in a well-organized underground nest with many other ants. A small mound of dirt usually reveals the entrance to the nest. This common ant also nests in rotten wood. The workers can be seen around-the-clock carrying morsels of food back to their nest-mates.

LOOK FOR: A smooth, slender, shiny, black or brown body and "waist" (pedicel, between the thorax and abdomen) with one segment. The antennae have 12 segments.

LENGTH: ⅟₁₆–¼".

HABITAT: Fields, yards, houses.

RANGE: Widespread except Pacific Northwest.

Like ants, Honeybees are
social insects. They live in
huge, organized colonies of
worker females and males,
headed by one queen bee.
These bees produce the honey
that we eat. They are also
pollinators of many fruit and
vegetable crops.

LOOK FOR. A slender, hairy bee;
brownish thorax is the hairiest
part; the abdomen has orange-
yellow and black bands.
"Baskets" for carrying pollen are
on hind legs.

LENGTH: ⅜–⅝".

HABITAT: Woods, fields, gardens.

RANGE: Widespread.

CAUTION: May sting.

AMERICAN BUMBLEBEE
Bombus pennsylvanicus

LOOK FOR: A large, fuzzy, black and yellow-
orange bee; dark wings. Gathers nectar;
attacks if nest disturbed. **LENGTH:** ⅞".
HABITAT: Woods, gardens, meadows. **RANGE:**
Widespread. **CAUTION:** Painful sting.

AMERICAN HOVER FLY
Metasyrphus americanus

LOOK FOR: A black fly with yellow bands
on abdomen that make it look like a
Honeybee. Wings are clear. **LENGTH:** ¼–¾".
HABITAT: Woods, fields, gardens. **RANGE:**
Widespread.

COMMON CARPENTER BEE
Xylocopoides virginica

LOOK FOR: A metallic blue-black body; less
hairy than American Bumblebee and no
yellow bands. **LENGTH:** 1". **HABITAT:** Woods,
farms, suburbs. **RANGE:** East.

BLACK-AND-YELLOW GARDEN SPIDER
Argiope aurantia

The Black-and-yellow Garden Spider spins a web with a vertical zigzag pattern in the center, where the female often sits, head downward. The male builds his web in the outer portions of the female's.

GOLDENROD SPIDER
(CRAB SPIDER)
Misumena vatia

LOOK FOR: Female is yellow to white with red streaks on each side of the abdomen; a reddish-brown spot is between the eyes. Also called Flower Spider. **LENGTH:** ⅜". **HABITAT:** Meadows, fields, and gardens on white or yellow flowers. **RANGE:** Widespread.

GREEN LYNX SPIDER
Peucetia viridans

LOOK FOR: Bright green, cream, or tan body; legs are yellow with black spines. **LENGTH:** ⅝". **HABITAT:** Fields, woods. **RANGE:** Southern United States.

LOOK FOR: Bold yellow-and-black markings on large egg-shaped abdomen; long, hairy legs with yellow-and-black bands.

LENGTH: ¼–1⅛".

HABITAT: Meadows, gardens.

RANGE: Widespread.

139

BLACK WIDOW SPIDER
Latrodectus mactans

AMERICAN HOUSE SPIDER
Achaearanea tepidariorum

LOOK FOR: A round, yellowish-brown body streaked with black and gray. **LENGTH:** ¼". **HABITAT:** Houses, barns, other buildings. **RANGE:** Widespread.

The female Black Widow Spider waits upside down on her ragged web, guarding her egg sac and flashing her red warning mark. She will attack anything that approaches her web, and her bite can be fatal. The male does not bite.

LOOK FOR. A glossy black spider. The female's abdomen is almost round with a red hourglass pattern on the underside. The male is smaller, marked with red and white along the sides.

LENGTH: Female: ⅜". Male: ⅛".

HABITAT: Piles of wood, brush, or trash; cellars.

RANGE: Most common in the South; can be found north to Kansas and Massachusetts.

CAUTION: Poisonous bite.

METAPHID JUMPING SPIDER
Metaphidippus spp.

LOOK FOR: Lots of hairs give this spider its grayish color. **LENGTH:** ¼". **HABITAT:** Meadows, woods, fences. **RANGE:** Widespread.

BROWN DADDY-LONG-LEGS
Phalangium opilio

LOOK FOR: Reddish-brown body with four pairs of long, thread-like legs. **LENGTH:** ⅛–¼". **HABITAT:** Woods, fields. **RANGE:** Widespread.

141

CAROLINA WOLF SPIDER
Hogna carolinensis

NURSERY WEB SPIDER
Pisaurina mira

LOOK FOR: Golden brown; may have band along middle of back. **LENGTH:** ⅝". **HABITAT:** Fields, woods, houses. **RANGE:** East Coast to Minnesota and Texas.

DESERT TARANTULA
Aphonopelma chalcodes

LOOK FOR: Head and thorax grayish brown; abdomen brown-black, hairy. **LENGTH:** 2–2¾". **HABITAT:** Desert. **RANGE:** Southwest. **CAUTION:** Will bite if provoked but bite not fatal.

GRASS SPIDER
Agelenopsis spp.

LOOK FOR: Head and thorax yellowish with center stripe; dark and light bands on sides. **LENGTH:** ¾". **HABITAT:** Grassy areas, shrubs, buildings. **RANGE:** Widespread.

The Carolina Wolf Spider does not spin a web. It is a nighttime hunter and scurries along the ground. The female carries her spiderlings on her back for weeks or months until it is time for them to scatter.

LOOK FOR: A gray-brown body with a dark center stripe on the abdomen; long, hairy legs; eight large, dark eyes of unequal size.

LENGTH: ¾–1⅛".

HABITAT: Fields.

RANGE: Widespread.

GIANT DESERT HAIRY SCORPION
Hadrurus arizonensis

Scorpions look a bit like miniature lobsters, but they have something lobsters don't: a poison-tipped tail for stinging prey (mostly insects), other scorpions, and enemies. They generally don't sting people, but will if disturbed. The sting is painful and in some species fatal. A female scorpion carries her babies on her back for 10–15 days before they go off on their own.

LOOK FOR: A dark body and pale yellow legs, claws, and tail. Stinger at tip of tail; body and tail divided into segments; pincer-like claws.

LENGTH: 5½".

HABITAT: Deserts.

RANGE: Southwest.

CAUTION: Painful sting, not fatal.

CENTRUROIDES SCORPION
Centruroides spp.

LOOK FOR: Tan body, often with a greenish-yellow stripe. **LENGTH:** 2¼".
HABITAT: Under logs, stones; in ground litter; on dirt roads. **RANGE:** South and Southwest. **CAUTION:** Sting can be fatal.

GIANT VINEGARONE
Mastigoproctus giganteus

LOOK FOR: Brownish-black body. Curled, thread-like tail. Also called Grampus.
LENGTH: 3⅛". **HABITAT:** Soil, under logs, humid buildings. **RANGE:** South and Southwest. **CAUTION:** Painful pinch.

PALE WINDSCORPION
Eremobates pallipes

LOOK FOR: Tan body, with gray-green on back. Pincer-like claws on first pair of legs.
LENGTH: ⅝–1¼". **HABITAT:** Arid, semiarid areas. **RANGE:** West, Southwest, Canadian southwest. **CAUTION:** Stings.

145

EASTERN WOOD TICK
Dermacentor variabilis

The Wood Tick, also known as the "Dog Tick," waits on low leaves for passing mammals (especially deer). It buries its head in the animal's flesh and extracts blood. As it feeds, it expands, dropping off after it is fully engorged. This tick can spread diseases. If you are bitten, avoid infection by carefully removing both the tick's body and head. This species does not transmit Lyme disease.

LOOK FOR: Female is reddish-brown with silvery shield near small, orangish head; brown legs. Male is pale gray with reddish-brown spots on legs.

LENGTH: ⅛".

HABITAT: Woods, shrubs, tall grass.

RANGE: Widespread in the East.

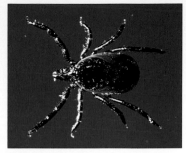

DEER TICK
Ixodes dammini

LOOK FOR: Adult: reddish brown, oval-shaped. Larva and nymph: the size of a pinhead. Carried by deer and mice. **LENGTH:** ⅟₁₆". **HABITAT:** Brushy fields, woods. **RANGE:** Northeast, upper Midwest, Pacific Coast. **CAUTION.** Transmits Lyme disease to humans.

VELVET MITE
Trombidium spp.

LOOK FOR: Fuzzy red mite; oval-to-round shape. Adults eat insect eggs, which helps to control the insect population. **LENGTH:** ⅛". **HABITAT:** Plants and soil in moist woods. **RANGE:** Widespread.

147

HOUSE CENTIPEDE
Scutigera coleoptrata

This centipede is scary-looking but relatively harmless, except of course to the insects it eats. Centipedes don't necessarily have 100 legs; some species have only 15 pairs, while others have more than 170 pairs!

LOOK FOR: A light brown, fast-moving centipede. It has strong jaws and two long antennae. One pair of legs per body segment (15 pairs in all).

LENGTH: 4".

HABITAT: Leaf litter, dead trees, cellars.

RANGE: Widespread.

CAUTION: Bites; some species are poisonous.

MILLIPEDE
Narceus spp.

LOOK FOR: Slow-moving vegetarian with about 100 pairs of legs, two pairs of legs per segment. Rolls into a spiral ball when threatened. Releases a foul smell to repel predators. **LENGTH:** 4".
HABITAT: Meadows, woods. **RANGE:** Widespread.

SOWBUG (WOODLICE/PILLBUG)
Armadillium vulgare

LOOK FOR: Gray, rounded, oval body with shrimp-like body plates; seven pairs of legs. Rolls into a ball when threatened.
LENGTH: ½". **HABITAT:** Under rocks, logs.
RANGE: Widespread.

149

How to use the reference section

Spicebush Swallowtail

The **Glossary** below contains terms used by naturalists and entomologists. Look up words you don't know here. Following the glossary are insect **Resources**—books, tapes, CDs, and organizations. Finally, there is an **Index** of species covered in the field guide, listing both common and scientific names.

Abdomen
The hind end of an insect's or spider's body.

Antenna
A feeler on an insect's head. An insect has two antennae and uses them to smell and touch things.

Arachnid
An arthropod with eight legs, no antennae, and a body that is usually divided into two sections. Spiders, scorpions, ticks, and mites are arachnids.

Arthropod
An animal with an outer skeleton (exoskeleton) and jointed legs. Insects, spiders, centipedes, and lobsters are all arthropods.

Cephalothorax
The front part of a spider's two-part body. It consists of both the head and thorax, which are separate body parts in an insect.

Chrysalis
A butterfly pupa. A caterpillar turns into a chrysalis before becoming an adult butterfly.

Complete Metamorphosis
A process of development that takes place in four stages: egg, larva, pupa, adult. The larva looks very different from the adult.

Compound eyes
Eyes that are made up of a number of smaller units. Each unit has it own lens.

Dung
Animal droppings.

Elytra
The two hard front wings of a beetle or an earwig.

Entomologist
A scientist who studies insects.

Evolve
To change gradually over a long period of time.

Exoskeleton
An arthropod's tough outer covering. It supports and protects the animal's soft inner body.

Eyespots
A pattern of scales on the wing of a moth or butterfly

that resembles an eye and helps to startle predators.

Family
A division of the animal or plant kingdom, below an order and above a genus.

Fore wings
The front pair of wings of an insect. In some insects the front wings cover the hind wings and are called wing covers.

Fossils
Remains or traces of prehistoric plants or animals.

Generation
The young that hatch from a female's batch of eggs.

Genus
A division of the plant or animal kingdom, below a family and above a species.

Gradual (Incomplete) Metamorphosis
A process of development that takes place in three stages: egg, nymph (or naiad), and adult.

Invertebrate
An animal without a backbone, such as an insect or a lobster.

Larva
A young insect in the stage of growth that comes

between egg and pupa.

Mandibles
A pair of jaws used by an insect for grasping and chewing.

Molt
To shed the skin.

Naiad
A nymph that lives underwater. Mayflies, dragonflies, and damselflies spend much of their lives as naiads.

Nocturnal
Active at night.

Nymph
A young insect that lacks wings and lives on land.

Pedicel
A thin body part that links the abdomen to the thorax in some insects, and the abdomen to the cephalothorax in spiders.

Phylum
A major division of the animal kingdom. Insects belong to a phylum called Arthropoda.

Pollinate
To carry the pollen of one flower to another flower.

Proboscis
A long, thin set of mouthparts used for

reaching or piercing a source of food.

Pronotum
The shield-like top of the first section of an insect's thorax.

Pupa
A stage of insect growth in between the larval stage and the adult form. The pupa is not active.

Segmented
Divided into sections or parts.

Species
A division of the animal or plant kingdom that is below a genus. Animals belonging to the same species can mate and produce young.

Spp.
Refers to several similar species in the same genus.

Tarsus
An insect's "foot"—the last part of one of its legs.

Thorax
The middle section of an insect's three-part body. The wings and legs are attached to the thorax.

Vertebrate
An animal with a backbone.

RESOURCES

FOR FURTHER READING

Amazing Insects
(Eyewitness Juniors Series)
Laurence Mound and Frank
Greenaway (Photographer)
Alfred A. Knopf, 1993

Bees, Wasps, and Ants
(Golden Guide Series)
George S. Fichter and Kristin
Kest (Illustrator)
Golden Books, 1993

**The Book of Spiders and
Scorpions**
Rod Preston-Mafham
Barnes & Noble Books, 1991

Bugs
(Incredible Insects Series)
James E. Gerholdt
Abdo & Daughters Publishing,
1996

Bugs!
(Rookie Reader Series)
Patricia and Fredrick McKissack
Children's Press, 1988

Dung beetle

**Bugs: A Closer Look at the
World's Tiny Creatures**
Jinny Johnson
Reader's Digest Kids, 1995

Bugs & Other Insects
Bobbie Kalman
Crabtree Publishing, 1994

Butterflies and Moths
John Feltwell
Dorling Kindersley, 1993

Extremely Weird Insects
Sarah Lovett
John Muir Publications,
1992

**The Fascinating World of
Ants**
Angels Julivert
Barron's, 1991

Insect
(Eyewitness Juniors Series)
Laurence Mound
Alfred A. Knopf, 1990

Insect Lives
(Ranger Rick Science
Spectacular Series)
Melvin Berger
Newbridge Communications,
1996

**Insect Metamorphosis: From
Egg to Adult**
Ron and Nancy Goor
Simon & Schuster, 1990

Insect Study
Boy Scouts of America, 1985

Insects
(Eyewitness Explorers Series)
Steve Parker
Dorling Kindersley, 1992

Insects
(Golden Guide Series)
Clarence Cottam and
Herbert S. Zim
Golden Books, 1987

Insects of North America
Dr. George C. McGavin and

Richard Lewington (Illustrator)
Thunder Bay Press, 1995

Journey to the Ants
Bert Holldobler and
Edward O. Wilson
Belknap Press, 1994

**National Audubon Society Field
Guide to North American
Butterflies**
Robert Michael Pyle
Alfred A. Knopf, 1981

**National Audubon Society Field
Guide to North American Insects
& Spiders**
Lorus and Margery Milne
Alfred A. Knopf, 1980

**National Audubon Society
Pocket Guide to Familiar
Butterflies of North America**
Richard K. Walton
Alfred A. Knopf, 1990

**National Audubon Society
Pocket Guide to Insects
and Spiders**
John Farrand, Jr.
Alfred A. Knopf, 1988

**Peterson First Guide to
Butterflies and Moths**
Paul A. Opler
Houghton Mifflin, 1994

**Peterson First Guide to
Caterpillars of North America**
Amy Bartlett Wright
Houghton Mifflin, 1993

**Peterson First Guide to
Insects of North America**
Christopher Leahy
Houghton Mifflin, 1987

**Simon & Schuster Children's
Guide to Insects and Spiders**
Jinny Johnson
Simon & Schuster, 1996

What Is an Insect?
Robert Snedden
Sierra Club Books for Children,
1997

The Young Naturalist
Andrew Mitchell
Usborne Publishing Ltd.,
1989

TAPES AND DISKS

Bugs
Reading Rainbow,
Lancit Media Productions,
1988

**Predators of the Wild,
Vol. 9: Giant Tarantula**
Time/Warner Video, 1993

**See How They Grow: Insects
and Spiders**
Dorling Kindersley/
Sony Kids' Video, 1993

**Spiders: Webs of Steel
(Wildlife Tales)**
Capital Cities/ABC Video,
1990

Bug Adventure
Knowledge Adventure,
1994 (Windows/DOS)

Destination: Rainforest
Edmark, 1995
(Windows/Mac)

Hyperbug
Entomation
(Mac)

**Junior Nature Guide Series:
Insects**
ICE Inc.
(Windows/Mac)

The Multimedia Big Bug Book
Workman/Swift, 1995
(Windows/Mac)

ORGANIZATIONS

**American Entomological
Society Academy of
Natural Sciences**
1900 Ben Franklin Parkway
Philadelphia, PA 19103
Tel: 215-561-3978

National Audubon Society
700 Broadway
New York, NY 10003
1-800-274-4201
http://www.audubon.org/

National Wildlife Federation
1625 Tyson Drive
Winchester, VA 22603 0592
Tel: 540-722-4000
http://www.igc.apc.org/nwf/index

**North American Butterfly
Association**
4 Delaware Road
Morristown, NJ 07960
Tel: 973-285-0908

**Young Entomologist Society,
Inc.**
1915 Peggy Place
Lansing, MI 48910-2553
Tel/Fax: 517-887-0499
http://www.tesser.com/minibeast
E-mail: yesbugs@aol.com

WEB SITES

Amazing Insects Project
http://www.minnetonka.k12.mn.us/
schools/groveland/insect.proj/insects.
html

Entomology (Biosciences)
http://www.colostate.edu/Depts/
Entomology/WWWVL-
Entomology.html

Entomology on World-Wide Web
http://www.colostate.edu/Depts/
Entomology/www_sites.html

Girls with a Monarch

Project Monarch Butterfly
http://ngp.ngpc.state.ne.us/
monarch/monarch.html

INDEX

A

Acanthocephala femorata, 73
Achaearanea tepidariorum, 141
Acheta domestica, 67
Achorutes nivicola, 101
Acrosternum hilare, 70
Actias luna, 124
Adalia bipunctata, 94
Admiral, Red, 119
Agelenopsis spp., 143
Alderfly, 83
Anasa tristis, 71
Anax junius, 52
Anopheles spp., 105
Ant, Black Carpenter, 135
Ant, Fire, 135
Ant, Little Black, 134
Antheraea polyphemus, 125
Anthocharis sara, 115
Anthonomus grandis, 98
Anurida maritima, 101
Apantesis ornata, 129
Aphid, Green Apple, 80
Aphis pomi, 80
Aphonopelma chalcodes, 143
Apiocera haruspex, 109
Apiomerus spp., 73
Apis mellifera, 136
Argiope aurantia, 138
Arilus cristatus, 73
Armadillium vulgare, 149
Asilidae, Family, 108
Azure, Spring, 116

B

Backswimmer, Common, 69
Bee, Common Carpenter, 137
Bee Assassin, 73
Bee Killer, 109

Beetles, Whirligig, 69
Billbug, Stored-grain, 99
Bittacomorpha clavipes, 103
Blatella germanica, 57
Blatta orientalis, 57
Bluet, Doubleday's, 55
Bombus pennsylvanicus, 137
Borer, Locust, 96
Boxelder Bug, 75
Bumblebee, American, 137

C

Cabbage Bug, Harlequin, 71
Caddisfly, Large, 83
Calliphora vomitoria, 111
Calopteron reticulatum, 93
Calopteryx maculata, 54
Calosoma spp., 85
Camponotus pennsylvanicus, 135
Canthon spp., 87
Carpocapsa saltitans, 123
Carrion Beetle, American, 93
Caterpillar Hunter, 85
Catocala amatrix, 130
Celastrina ladon, 116
Celithemis eponina, 53
Centipede, House, 148
Centruroides spp., 145
Chauliognathus pennsylvanicus, 97
Chironomus attenuatus, 105
Chrysochus auratus, 91
Chrysopa spp., 83
Chrysops spp., 107
Cicada, Grand Western, 77
Cicada, Periodical, 76
Cicindela formosa, 85
  sexguttata, 84
Cockroach, American, 56
Cockroach, German, 57

Cockroach, Oriental, 57
Colias philodice, 115
Conenose, Blood-sucking, 72
Cootie, 101
Copper, American, 117
Corydalus cornutus, 82
Crane Fly, 102
Crane Fly, Giant Western, 103
Crane Fly, Phantom, 103
Cricket, Field, 66
Cricket, House, 67
Cricket, Jerusalem, 67
Cricket, Snowy Tree, 67
Culex pipiens, 104
Cushion Scale, Cottony, 81

D

Daddy-long-legs, Brown, 141
Danaus plexippus, 118
Darner, Green, 52
Dendrobius mandibularis, 97
Dendroides spp., 93
Dermacentor variabilis, 146
Diapheromera femorata, 59
Dissosteira carolina, 63
Dobsonfly, Eastern, 82
Drake, Brown, 51

E

Eacles imperialis, 125
Enallagma doubledayii, 55
Epargyreus clarus, 120
Ephemera simulans, 51
Ephestia kuehniella, 123
Epimecis hortaria, 131
Eremobates pallipes, 145
Eurytides marcellus, 113

F

Fire Beetle, 93
Firefly, 92
Flea, Human, 100
Flea, Snow, 101
Fly, American Hover, 137
Fly, Biting Stable, 111
Fly, Black, 105
Fly, Blue Bottle, 111
Fly, Deer, 107
Fly, Flower-loving, 109
Fly, House, 110
Fly, Robber, 108
Fly, Tachinid, 111
Forktail, Eastern, 55

G

Gerris remigis, 68
Graphocephala coccinea, 78
Grasshopper, Differential, 62
Grasshopper, Green Valley, 63
Ground Beetle, Common Black, 86
Gryllus pennsylvanicus, 66
Gyrinidae, Family, 69

H

Hadrurus arizonensis, 144
Hairstreak, Gray, 117
Harvestfly, Dogday, 77
Hemaris diffinus, 127
  thysbe, 126
Hexagenia spp., 51
Hippodamia convergens, 95
Hogna carolinensis, 142
Holorusia rubiginosa, 103
Honeybee, 136
Hornet, Bald-faced, 133
Horse Fly, American, 106
Horse Fly, Black, 107

Hyalophora cecropia, 125
Hylephila phyleus, 121
Hyles lineata, 127

I

Icerya purchasi, 81
Ichneumonidae, Family, 133
Ischnura verticalis, 55
Isia isabella, 129
Ixodes dammini, 147

J

Japanese Beetle, 90
Jewelwing, Ebony, 54
June Beetle, Ten-lined, 91
June bug, 91

K

Katydid, California, 63
Katydid, Fork-tailed Bush, 65
Katydid, True, 64

L

Lacewing, Green, 83
Ladybug Beetle, Convergent, 95

Ladybug Beetle, Two-spotted, 94
Lampyridae, Family, 92
Latrodectus mactans, 140
Leaf Beetle, Dogbane, 91
Leaf-footed Bug, Florida, 73
Leafhopper, Scarlet-and-green, 78
Leather-wing, Pennsylvania, 97
Leptocoris, Genus 75
Lethocerus americanus, 69
Libellula lydia, 53
  saturata, 53
Limenitis archippus, 119
Locust, Carolina, 63
Longhorn, Long-jawed, 97
Louse, Human Body, 101
Lucanus elephus, 88
Lycaena phlaeas, 117
Lygaeus kalmii, 74
Lymantria dispar, 128

M

Magicicada spp., 76
Malacosoma californicum, 129

Fork-tailed Bush Katydid
page 65

INDEX

Manduca quinquemaculata, 127
Mantid, Carolina, 59
Mantis, Praying, 58
Mantis religiosa, 58
Mastigoproctus giganteus, 145
May Beetle, 91
Mayfly, Brown Stream, 50
Mayfly, Golden, 51
Mealworm Beetle, Yellow, 87
Mealybug, Long-tailed, 81
Megacyllene robiniae, 96
Melanoplus differentialis, 62
Metaphidippus spp., 141
Metasyrphus americanus, 137
Microcentrum californicum, 65
Midge, Common, 105
Milkweed Beetle, Red, 95
Milkweed Bug, Large, 75
Milkweed Bug, Small, 74
Millipede, 149
Misumena vatia, 139
Mite, Velvet, 147
Monarch, 118
Monomorium minimum, 134
Mosquito, House, 104
Mosquito, Malaria-carrying, 105
Moth, Armyworm, 131

Moth, Bumblebee, 127
Moth, Cecropia, 125
Moth, Clothes, 123
Moth, Gypsy, 128
Moth, Hummingbird, 126
Moth, Imperial, 125
Moth, Indian Meal, 122
Moth, Luna, 124
Moth, Mexican Jumping Bean, 123
Moth, Mill, 123
Moth, Ornate Tiger, 129
Moth, Polyphemus, 125
Moth, Tomato Hornworm, 127
Moth, Western Tent Caterpillar, 129
Moth, Woolly Bear Caterpillar, 129
Mourning Cloak, 119
Murgantia histrionica, 71
Musca domestica, 110

N

Narceus spp., 149
Net-wing, Banded, 93
Notonecta undulata, 69
Nymphalis antiopa, 119

O

Odontotaenius disjunctus, 89
Oecanthus fultoni, 67
Oncometopia nigricans, 79
Oncopeltus fasciatus, 75

P

Papilio glaucus, 112
  polyxenes, 113
  zelicaon, 113
Patent-leather Beetle, 89
Pediculus humanus, 101
Pennant, Halloween, 53
Periplaneta americana, 56
Perlidae, Family, 60
Perlodidae, Family, 61
Peucetia viridans, 139
Phalangium opilio, 141
Phryganeidae, Family, 83
Phyllophaga spp., 91
Pieris napi, 115
  rapae, 114
Pillbug, 149
Pisaurina mira, 143
Platycotis vittata, 79
Plodia interpunctella, 122
Polistes spp., 133
Polyphylla decimlineata, 91

Carolina
Wolf
Spider

page 142

Popilla japonica, 90
Promachus fitchii, 109
Pseudalatia unipunctata, 131
Pseudococcus adonidum, 81
Pteronarcidae, Family, 61
Pterophylla camellifolia, 64
Pterostichus spp., 86
Pulex irritans, 100
Pyrgus communis, 121

R

Reticulitermes hesperus, 135
Rhithrogena spp., 50
Rhynchites bicolor, 99

S

Sara Orangetip, 115
Schistocerca shoshone, 63
Scorpion, Centruroides, 145
Scorpion, Giant Desert
   Hairy, 144
Scudderia furcata, 65
Scutigera coleoptrata, 148
Sharpshooter, 79
Sialis spp., 83
Silophilus granarius, 99
Silpha americana, 93
Simulium spp., 105
Sinodendron rugosum, 89
Skimmer, Red, 53
Skipper, Common
   Checkered, 121
Skipper, Fiery, 121
Skipper, Long-tailed, 121
Skipper, Silver-spotted,
   120
Solenopsis geminata, 135
Sowbug, 149
Sphinx, White-lined, 127
Spider, American House,
   141
Spider, Black-and-yellow
   Garden, 138
Spider, Black Widow, 140

Spider, Carolina Wolf,
   142
Spider, Crab, 139
Spider, Goldenrod, 139
Spider, Grass, 143
Spider, Green Lynx, 139
Spider, Metaphid
   Jumping, 141
Spider, Nursery Web, 143
Springtail, Seashore, 101
Squash Bug, 71
Stag Beetle, Elephant, 88
Stag Beetle, Rugose, 89
Stagmomantis carolina, 59
Stenopelmatus fuscus, 67
Stink Bug, Green, 70
Stomoxys calcitrans, 111
Stonefly, Common, 60
Stonefly, Giant, 61
Stonefly, Green winged, 61
Strider, Common Water,
   68
Strymon melinus, 117
Sulphur, Clouded, 115
Swallowtail, Anise, 113
Swallowtail, Black, 113
Swallowtail, Eastern Tiger,
   112
Swallowtail, Zebra, 113
Sweetheart Underwing,
   130

T

Tabanus americanus, 106
   atratus, 107
Tachinidae, Family, 111
Tarantula, Desert, 143
Tenebrio molitor, 87
Termite, Subterranean,
   135
Tetraopes tetraophthalmus, 95
Thripidae, Family, 81
Thrips, Common, 81
Tibicen canicularis, 77
   dorsata, 77

Tick, Deer, 147
Tick, Eastern Wood, 146
Tiger Beetle, Beautiful, 85
Tiger Beetle, Six-spotted
   Green, 84
Tineidae, Family, 123
Tipula spp., 102
Treehopper, Oak, 79
Triatoma sanguisuga, 72
Trombidium spp., 147
Tulip Tree Beauty, 131
Tumblebug, 87

U

Urbanus proteus, 121

V

Vanessa atalanta, 119
Vespula maculata, 133
   spp., 132
Viceroy, 119
Vinegarone, Giant, 145

W

Walkingstick, Northern,
   59
Wasp, Ichneumon, 133
Wasp, Paper, 133
Water Bug, Giant, 69
Weevil, Boll, 98
Weevil, Granary, 99
Weevil, Rose, 99
Wheel Bug, 73
White, Cabbage, 114
White, Mustard, 115
Whitetail, Common, 53
Windscorpion, Pale, 145
Woodlice, 149

X

Xylocopoides virginica, 137

Y

Yellow Jacket, 132

PHOTO/ILLUSTRATION CREDITS

Photo credits are listed by page from left to right, top to bottom.

Front cover (Praying Mantis): Michael Lustbader/Photo Researchers*
Half-title page (Monarch): M. H. Sharp/Photo Researchers
Title page (Regal Moth caterpillar): Norm Thomas/Photo Researchers
Table of contents (Long-jawed Longhorn): Betty Randall
6: Rick Cech
8a: Science Photo Library/Photo Researchers
8b: Lawrence Migdale/Photo Researchers
9: Joe DiStefano/Photo Researchers
10a: Gregory K. Scott/Photo Researchers
10b: Anthony Mercieca/Photo Researchers
11: L. West/Photo Researchers
12–13 (background): Gary Retherford/Photo Researchers
12a: Brian Kenney
12b: Scott Camazine/Photo Researchers
12c: Dr. Paul Zahl/Photo Researchers
13a: Robert Noonan/Photo Researchers
13b: Gary Retherford/Photo Researchers
14: John M. Coffman
15a: Byron Jorjorian
15b (scorpion): Rod Planck
15c: Ron Austing
15d: Brian Kenney
15e: Andrew J. Martinez/Photo Researchers
16a: Rod Planck
16b: James H. Robinson
17a: Brian Kenney
17b: Ray Coleman/Photo Researchers
18a: Joe Warfel
18b: Harry Rogers/Photo Researchers
19: Jim Roetzel
20–21 (background): Brian Kenney
20a: Brian Kenney
20b (cockroach): E. R. Degginger/Color-Pic, Inc.
20c: Michael P. Gadomski/Photo Researchers
21a: Brian Kenney
21b: Scott Camazine
21c: Brian Kenney
22–23 (background): Jim Roetzel
22a: Charles W. Melton
22b: Jim Roetzel
22c: Jim Roetzel

23a: J. H. Robinson/Photo Researchers
23b: Peter Hartlove
23c: John Serrao
23c: C. W. Brown/Photo Researchers
24a: Harry Rogers/Photo Researchers
24b: J. H. Robinson/Photo Researchers
24–25 (hercules beetle): J. H. Robinson/Photo Researchers
25a: Stephen Dalton/Photo Researchers
25b: A. H. Rider/Photo Researchers
26a: Brian Kenney
26b: Andrew Syred/SPL/Photo Researchers
27a: Nuridsany & Pérennou/Photo Researchers
27b: Andrew Syred/SPL/Photo Researchers
27c: L. West/Photo Researchers
28a: John Mitchell/Photo Researchers
28b: Brian Kenney
29a: Rob Curtis/The Early Birder
29b: Jeff Lepore/Photo Researchers
30a: Brian Kenney
30b: Charles W. Melton
31a: L. West/Photo Researchers
31b: Phillip Roullard
31c: James H. Robinson
32–33 (background): Scott Camazine/Photo Researchers
32a: Peter G. Aitken/Photo Researchers
32b: Joe Warfel
33: Scott Camazine/Photo Researchers
34: James H. Robinson
34–35: David Liebman
35: Stephen Dalton/Photo Researchers
36a: C. K. Lorenz/Photo Researchers
36b: James C. Godwin
37a: Rod Planck/Photo Researchers
37b: John Bova/Photo Researchers
37c: G. Penner/Okapia/Photo Researchers
38a: Brian Kenney
38b: Gregory G. Dimijian/Photo Researchers
38c: Brian Kenney
38d: Brian Kenney
38–39 (pipevine): Brian Kenney
39a: Rob & Ann Simpson
39b: Rod Planck
40a: Scott Camazine/Photo Researchers
40b: Rod Planck

40c: John Mitchell/Photo Researchers
41a: M. H. Sharp/Photo Researchers
41b: M. H. Sharp/Photo Researchers
41c: M. H. Sharp/Photo Researchers
41d: M. H. Sharp/Photo Researchers
41e: John Mitchell/Photo Researchers
41f: John Mitchell/Photo Researchers
42a: J. H. Robinson/Photo Researchers
42b: R. J. Erwin/Photo Researchers
42–43 (mantis): Michael Lustbader/Photo Researchers
43: Brian Kenney
44a: Jeff Ripple
44b: Rob Curtis/The Early Birder
44–45 (tarantula): Rob & Ann Simpson
45a: E. R. Degginger/Color-Pic, Inc.
45b: J. H. Robinson/Photo Researchers
46–47 (background): Dennis Frates
46a: A. H. Rider/Photo Researchers
46b: L. West/Photo Researchers
46–47 (silverspot): Paul A. Opler
47: Blair Nikula
48a: John M. Coffman
48b: John M. Coffman
50: Byron Jorjorian
51a: Peter Miller/Photo Researchers
51b: Brian Kenney
52: Jim Roetzel
53a: John Mitchell/Photo Researchers
53b: Rick Cech
53c: Lawrence E. Naylor/Photo Researchers
54: Joe McDonald/Visuals Unlimited
55a: James C. Godwin
55b: Sidney W. Dunkle
56: E. R. Degginger/Color-Pic, Inc.
57a: E. R. Degginger/Color-Pic, Inc.
57b: James H. Robinson
58: Andrew J. Martinez/Photo Researchers
59a: E. R. Degginger/Color-Pic, Inc.
59b: E. R. Degginger/Color-Pic, Inc.
60: Michael P. Gadomski/Photo Researchers
61a: Edward S. Ross
61b: Alan & Linda Detrick
62: E. R. Degginger/Color-Pic, Inc.
63a: E. R. Degginger/Color-Pic, Inc.
63b: Rod Planck
64: R. J. Erwin/Photo Researchers
65a: James P. Rowan
65b: Joe DiStefano/Photo Researchers
66: James H. Robinson
67a: James H. Robinson
67b: Joe Warfel
67c: David Liebman
68: E. R. Degginger/Color-Pic, Inc.
69a: Stephen Dalton/Photo Researchers
69b: Bill Johnson
69c: E. R. Degginger/Color-Pic, Inc.
70: Brian Kenney

71a: Harry Rogers/Photo Researchers
71b: Scott Camazine/Photo Researchers
72: Brian Kenney
73a: Brian Kenney
73b: M. H. Sharp/Photo Researchers
73c: Brian Kenney
74: Harry Rogers/Photo Researchers
75a: Charles W. Melton
75b: Brian Kenney
76: Rob & Ann Simpson
77a: Edward S. Ross
77b: Rob Curtis/The Early Birder
78: Rod Planck
79a: Brian Kenney
79b: Brian Kenney
80: E. R. Degginger/Color-Pic, Inc.
81a: J. H. Robinson/Photo
　Researchers
81b: Scott Camazine/Photo
　Researchers
81c: Alan & Linda Detrick
82: John M. Coffman
83a: L. West/Photo Researchers
83b: L. West/Photo Researchers
83c: Brian Kenney
84: Joe Warfel
85a: Rod Planck
85b: James H. Robinson
86: Joe DiStefano/Photo
　Researchers
87a: Gilbert Grant/Photo
　Researchers
87b: B. B. Jones/Photo
　Researchers
88: E. R. Degginger/Photo
　Researchers
89a: Edward S. Ross
89b: Roger Rageot/David Liebman Stock
90: Michael Lustbader/Photo
　Researchers
91a: Scott Camazine/Photo
　Researchers
91b: David Liebman
91c: Rob Curtis/The Early Birder
92: James R. Fisher/Photo Researchers
93a: Scott Camazine/Photo Researchers
93b: Edward S. Ross
93c: Brian Kenney
94: Bill Johnson
95a: John M. Coffman
95b: James H. Robinson
96: Stephen P. Parker/Photo
　Researchers
97a: Betty Randall
97b: Alan & Linda Detrick
98: E. R. Degginger/Photo
　Researchers
99a: Stephen Dalton/Photo
　Researchers
99b: Noah Poritz/Photo
　Researchers

100: M. I. Walker/Anthony Bannister
　Photo Library/Photo Researchers
101a: Joe Warfel
101b: Kjell B. Sandved/Photo
　Researchers
101c: Biophoto Associates/Photo
　Researchers
102: Brian Kenney
103a: Stephen P. Parker/Photo
　Researchers
103b: E. R. Degginger/Color-Pic, Inc.
104: L. West/Photo Researchers
105a: Stephen Dalton/Photo
　Researchers
105b: Edward S. Ross
105c: L. West/Photo Researchers
106: James H. Robinson
107a: Brian Kenney
107b: E. R. Degginger/Color-Pic, Inc.
108: Rod Planck
109a: Edward S. Ross
109b: Brian Kenney
110: James H. Robinson
111a: Brian Kenney
111b: E. R. Degginger/Photo
　Researchers
111c: Rod Planck
112: Rick Cech
113a: Thomas C. Boyden
113b: Brian Kenney
113c: E. R. Degginger/Color-Pic, Inc.
114: E. R. Degginger/Color-Pic, Inc.
115a: James P. Rowan
115b: David Liebman
115c: Thomas C. Boyden
116: Rick Cech
117a: Brian Kenney
117b: Rick Cech
118: E. R. Degginger/Color-Pic, Inc.
119a: Thomas C. Boyden
119b: Rick Cech
119c: Joe Warfel
120: E. R. Degginger/Color-Pic, Inc.
121a: Rick Cech
121b: Rick Cech
121c: Brian Kenney
122: Stephen Dalton/Photo
　Researchers
123a: Treat Davidson/Photo
　Researchers
123b: Stephen Dalton/Photo
　Researchers
123c: Edward S. Ross
124: Stephen G. Maka
125a: Rod Planck
125b: Brian Kenney
125c: Tom Vezo
126: Brian Kenney
127a: Rob & Ann Simpson
127b: Hugh Spenser/Photo
　Researchers

127c: Thomas C. Boyden
128: E. R. Degginger/Color-Pic, Inc.
129a: Charles W. Melton
129b: David Liebman
129c: Allen Blake Sheldon
130: E. R. Degginger/Color-Pic, Inc.
131a: John Bova/Photo Researchers
131b: Jeff Lepore/Photo Researchers
132: Rob Curtis/The Early Birder
133a: James H. Robinson
133b: E. R. Degginger/Color-Pic, Inc.
133c: Rod Planck
134: Bill Johnson
135a: James H. Robinson
135b: E. R. Degginger/Color-Pic, Inc.
135c: James H. Robinson
136: Lance Beeny
137a: Brian Kenney
137b: E. R. Degginger/Color-Pic, Inc.
137c: E. R. Degginger/Color-Pic, Inc.
138: Jim Roetzel
139a: Peter Harlove
139b: Joe Warfel
140: James H. Robinson
141a: E. R. Degginger/Color-Pic, Inc.
141b: Rod Planck
141c: Rob & Ann Simpson
142: Mark Smith
143a: Nuridsany & Pérennou/Photo
　Researchers
143b: Rob & Ann Simpson
143c: E. R. Degginger/Color-Pic, Inc.
144: Robert E. Barber
145a: Brian Kenney
145b: Brian Kenney
145c: Rod Planck
146: James H. Robinson
147a: E. R. Degginger/Color-Pic, Inc.
147b: David Liebman
148: James P. Rowan
149a: Brian Kenney
149b: Michael P. Gadomski/Photo
　Researchers
150: Rick Cech
152: Brian Kenney
153: Renee Lynn/Photo Researchers
155: John Mitchell/Photo Researchers
156: Mark Smith

*Photo Researchers, Inc.
60 East 56th Street
New York, NY 10022

Prepared and produced by
Chanticleer Press, Inc., and Chic Simple Design

Founder, Chanticleer Press, Inc.: Paul Steiner

Publisher, Chanticleer Press, Inc.: Andrew Stewart
Publishers, Chic Simple Design: Jeff Stone, Kim Johnson Gross

Chanticleer Staff:
Editor-in-Chief: Amy K. Hughes
Director of Production: Alicia Mills
Production Associate: Philip Pfeifer
Photo Editor: Zan Carter
Senior Editor: Lauren Weidenman
Managing Editors: Kristina Lucenko and Edie Locke
Editorial Assistant: Karin Murphy

Project Editors: Edward S. Barnard, Sharon Fass Yates
Bookmark Associates, Inc.

Chic Simple Design Staff:
Art Direction/Design: Takuyo Takahashi
Production/Design: Jinger Peissig
Project Coordinator: Gillian Oppenheim
Production: Camilla Marstrand
Design Interns: Kathryn Hammill, Danielle Huthart,
Diane Shaw, Sylvie Pusztaszeri

Writer (The world of insects, How to look at insects): Christina Wilsdon
Consultant: Brian Cassie, North American Butterfly Association
Copy Editors: Kristina Bohl, Sarah Burns
Illustrator: Taina Litwak
Icon Illustrator: Holly Kowitt
Studio Photographer: David Bashaw

Scholastic Inc. Staff:
Editorial Director: Wendy Barish, Creative Director: David Saylor,
Managing Editor: Manuela Soares,
Manufacturing Manager: Karen Fuchs

Original Series Design: Chic Simple Design, Takuyo Takahashi